The school fundraiser

David G Poppitt MSc

THE *QUESTIONS* PUBLISHING COMPANY LTD
BIRMINGHAM
2003

The Questions Publishing Company Ltd
321 Bradford Street, Digbeth, Birmingham B5 6ET

© David Poppitt 2001

Text and activity pages in this publication may be photocopied for use by the purchaser or in the purchasing institution only. Otherwise, all rights reserved and text may not be reprinted or reproduced or utilised in any form or by any electronic, mechanical or other means, now known or hereafter invented, including photocopying and recording, or in any information storage or retrieval system, without permission in writing from the publishers.

First published in 2001

ISBN: 1-84190-046-X

Cover design by Martin Cater/Ivan Morison
Ilustrations by Steve Chadburn
Printed in the UK

Contents

Summary iv

Introduction vi

*Chapter one: What we can and
can't do, and will the taxman help?*
A comparison with charitable fundraising 1
Charity law requirements 3
Tax incentives 10

Chapter two: The role of development
The first steps 17
Staffing of a development office 19
A relationship database 22
Building alumni relationships – an American experience 26
Legacies 30
Trusts and foundations 37
The telephone in fundraising for schools 41
The role of consultants in fundraising 45

Chapter three: Imaginative event management
How to organise a summer fete 56
A Christmas Bazaar 64
A jumble sale 64
Children and fundraising 66
Sporting events 72
Planning a charity sports event – some general points 75
Field sports events – points to remember 76
Route sports 77
Other sporting ideas 77
For the more adventurous 78
A final word on event management 86

Chapter four: The school as a business
Utilising school facilities 87

Appendix 1: Some useful addresses 111

Appendix 2: Useful reading 115

Summary

ANY MAJOR project requires associated income generation, either for matched or revenue funding purposes. Rosegarth Associates, including its principal consultant, David Poppitt, with over ten years, experience in the field and the responsibility of having raised over £12.5 million in the health and education sectors, offers help and advice to organisations needing to raise funds.

A prime understanding of legal requirements and codes of practice are necessary before any other steps are taken. The role of the trustees of charities and that of the headteacher and governors in schools is crucial to the success of any fundraising. A thorough understanding of tax and VAT elements is also essential and can greatly increase income.

With a long-term approach to relationship building and a concentration of 'friendraising' leading to fundraising, schools and charities can avoid the damaging effects of 'smash and grab' appeals over a short period. It is important that a professional approach be taken, with an understanding that some initial funding needs to be set aside for an office and personnel. It can be summarised briefly as 'speculate to accumulate'. A key element is the development of a relationship database containing as much information as possible about supporters of the cause and future donors. Networking opportunities abound via press and media contacts and, most importantly, word of mouth. Literature is also a key aspect to enable portrayal of your intent, as is the power of telephone fundraising.

The various methods of extracting money from different cohorts of potential donors involve a great variety of techniques and need to be considered alongside lottery applications, approaches to trusts and foundations, and potential legacies. Specialised approaches to the corporate sector involve a realisation of the importance of sponsorship and business partnerships, and can be coupled with event management and letting of facilities, creating community involvement and symbiotic relationships with local businesses.

Introduction

So, what's new? People have been raising money for centuries. Charity has been in existence ever since the first caveman offered his flint to his neighbour for him to be able to make a fire. It is more than likely that this came before he even thought of asking for something in return, i.e. trading. However, with today's modern communications and advanced technology, fundraising has had to become increasingly sophisticated in its own right. Charitable fundraising has had to adapt with time and to constantly search for original ideas and innovative techniques to make the actual cause more attractive than all the competitors. Charitable income, in general, now exceeds many of the major Plc organisations with figures in the £billions.

Until very recently, educational fundraising has played a minor role in the whole concept of charitable activities, where there has been a bias towards health, deprivation, third world and animal charities. The latter have concentrated on a major PR effort. How many people do you know, living in Birmingham, who have been rescued by lifeboat? Yet, the charity raises thousands of pounds in Birmingham to support the lifeboats. Schools have always concentrated solely on their primary users, i.e. the parents of the children, to raise money to support those extra books and facilities that, hopefully, will benefit their own children. While I do not decry these activities, this book will attempt to look at a broader fundraising approach to educational needs.

So, why me? I was brought up in a household of teaching with both my parents as members of the teaching profession. Though this may well have been the reason I did not join the profession myself, it was certainly the reason my own education took the course it did. My father was deputy headteacher at the local state grammar school and he was convinced that it would not be a good idea for me to attend the same school at which he taught. So I was entered for the examination to attend a well-thought-of local direct grant school – Bolton School. Though I did not realise it at the time, this was to be a significant step, which would influence future roles and, indeed, lead to my writing this book.

Following the basic O- and A-levels, introductions to the sports of rugby, cricket and swimming, and the opportunity to travel all over Europe, I went on to university and obtained a degree in biochemistry. On looking back, I wonder if I would have obtained the same broad aspect of education at another school. From university I entered the medical research laboratories at Christie Hospital, in Manchester, one of the leading cancer hospitals in Europe. My earliest introduction to fundraising came in the early seventies when I found myself talking about our work to volunteers who were raising money for research at the hospital.

A career of around twenty-one years in experimental chemotherapy saw me acquire a master's degree and publish a number of articles in medical research journals. This was coupled with a liaison role to the charitable fundraisers as I appeared to be able to communicate at all levels about the work – unlike, I'm afraid to say, many of my contemporaries. Towards the end of the eighties, the liaison role was becoming more significant and the hospital recognised the important aspects of public awareness and education about early presentation of cancer. To be brief, I bought a suit, they gave me an office and I changed role to one of full-time PR. As I spread the word about the hospital, people actually began to raise money for us, so it does not take too much imagination to see how I became a professional fundraiser.

As an aside, it is fascinating to look at the background of professional fundraisers, though extremely difficult to identify a common denominator apart from extroverts and sales technique. By far the most important thing for a fundraiser to do is to say out loud: "I am a professional fundraiser." I am fascinated by the way people now view me. As a medical research scientist I was on a pedestal as an expert in my field, and I was most often in a position where it was recognised that I knew far more about my subject than my audience. How that changed as a fundraiser! Immediately, everyone in the hospital, from the cleaners to the consultants, knew exactly what I should be doing and were more than ready to tell me at every opportunity. The same applies in schools, particularly among senior staff and governors. Sadly, as in medicine, a little knowledge is dangerous and can lead to disastrous results in fundraising with, for example, smash and grab appeals ruining long-term relationship building prospects for major donors.

From the onset of the new NHS Trust status of the Christie Hospital in 1991 we began to be proactive rather than reactive towards fundraising. I became the appeals director and by 1995 had fifteen staff and had taken the charitable income to £3 million per annum. Sadly I had become purely an administrator – plotting pie charts of what the staff were doing and constantly involved in performance review assessment. It was in these circumstances that I responded to Bolton School.

I had attended the school on a scholarship from the local educational authority. These were then known as direct grant scholarships and were in existence until 1976. They were replaced in 1979 by the assisted places scheme, which continued to give bright children from poor parental backgrounds the opportunity of an education at such a school. The governors at Bolton School, and particularly the chairman, Lord Robert Haslam, recognised the likelihood of a change of government leading to the abolition of the assisted places scheme and the importance both to the social mix within the school and to the financial aspects that this would bring. I was appointed to the role of full-time development director at the school in Easter 1995 in an attempt to address this potential problem that, of course, became reality on the election of the new government in May 1997. I left Bolton School at the end of 1998 to take on the role of full-time fundraising consultant. Much of the material within this book is based on my experiences at Bolton and with clients since leaving, in both the state and independent sectors, and will draw on case studies of actual activities undertaken with differing degrees of success.

Educational fundraising is usually covered beneath an umbrella called development. This also covers PR and marketing and is now called advancement in the USA. As I shall discuss later, there is much we can learn from the Americans, but we must be aware of the different culture here and many things that would work there will not work here. Development is gradually becoming recognised in schools as an increasingly important activity. The independent sector has led in this, mainly due to the existence of seed funds and the ability of the governors to be able to make decisions without having to refer to the bureaucratic structures often experienced within the state sector. However, as will be seen, the vast majority of techniques and methodology are equally applicable to Harrow and Westminster Schools as they are to the little church village primary school and the inner-city state comprehensive.

This book has been written following a series of articles that have appeared in *Resource Manager*, a supplement to the periodical *Managing Schools Today*. It is not intended to be an exhaustive guide to fundraising within schools, but rather a collection of ideas and techniques shown to have been successful in the recent past. It is not intended to replace any activities conducted by parents' associations or friends' groups, but can be seen to offer opportunities that will run in parallel with these or similar activities.

I would like to thank all the individuals who recognise that they may have contributed, willingly or otherwise, to the case studies represented.

**To my wife
Susie**

Chapter one

What we can and can't do, and will the taxman help?

A comparison with charitable fundraising

IT IS DIFFICULT to imagine any success being gained from a street or house-to-house collection in support of the local school. Whereas charities can appeal to the general public for their emotive purposes, schools have a much narrower target audience. In marketing terminology, charities aim many of their appeals, such as a direct mail, to a 'cold' audience, in some cases buying in mailing lists and spending much time and effort on formulating and writing appealing literature. On the other hand, schools have a 'warm' target audience of parents, alumni, staff and governors. Whereas literature is extremely important, a completely different approach is needed. Schools have another advantage in that they can go one step further than a purely philanthropic approach. As will be discussed later in much more detail, they have resources that they can offer and can portray themselves much more on a business level in any deal that could elicit financial support.

Charities and their fundraising methods can offer a great deal. I am sure many parent or teacher groups have promises auctions, car boot sales, race nights, antique and craft fairs, summer and Christmas fairs, sponsored events, non-uniform days, and so on. A glance at the local newspaper will reveal a multitude of ideas easily adaptable to raising money for the school. A company in Wigan, Lancashire, called 8th Wonder (01942 768815), has set up a splendid idea whereby it produces lapel badges based on the school logo or crest. These are available at a modest cost, mounted on cards, and can be issued to supporters for a donation. On no account can they be sold for a fixed price, as this constitutes trading. But the majority will donate at least £1.00 for a badge originally bought at less than half that price. Local incentives for children managing to raise the most money in such a fashion can lead to friendly rivalry and involvement, with parents distributing the badges to work colleagues and neighbours.

We have found this idea appeals particularly to children in Years 7 and 8. In a similar way this company has successfully been involved in fundraising within schools by supplying small beanie novelties, such as bears, hedgehogs and squirrels, or seasonal reindeer, or Father Christmases. Interestingly, this approach was one of the most successful adopted in community fundraising for the Christie Hospital, and is currently much utilised in the charitable field for creating employee fundraising initiatives within the corporate sector that can lead to employer matched funding.

Many schools are themselves involved in charitable fundraising for local and national charities. An interesting opportunity arises in this context for joint activities. At Bolton School we were particularly successful in organising an outdoor Shakespeare production within the beautiful grounds. This was held jointly with the local children's hospice. Hence, we were able to attract both the school family and the many supporters of the hospice to a most enjoyable event and spilt the proceeds fifty-fifty. Along similar lines it may be worth talking to local charities or branches of national charities, which are always looking for potential venues for events. It may also be worth discussing possibilities of joint Christmas cards and calendars. I know of a local charity that produces a calendar that is made up of children's paintings for each month. I see no reason why the school should not also benefit financially and help with distribution. I can see an immediate market for sales from parents and families of the children whose paintings are chosen.

Charity law requirements

The law is there to protect people and the charitable activities of an organisation. Whereas many typical fundraising activities taken up, such as those mentioned above in the context of Parents' Association (PA) activities, are not seriously considered as infringing on the legislation, care must be taken if further activities are contemplated along the lines discussed later. I refer to definite trading aspects.

There is no doubt that considerable advantage can be gained on taxation aspects by setting up a registered charity, and any school seriously contemplating raising funds should adopt this approach. Guidelines are available from the offices of the Charity Commissioner. It is usual either for a group of governors to become trustees of a new charity or for the school to set up a separate foundation. Alternatively, a PA or alumni group can set up a charity. It is extremely important, before embarking on this route, for the trustees to be aware of their legal responsibilities within the charity. These have changed considerably within the last decade and I advise legal consultation on this issue.

While raising money should be an enjoyable experience for all concerned, there are rules that govern the way money is collected and how it is handled thereafter. It is always wise before planning to take advice from all relevant parties. In some cases this will involve the relevant local authority or police department. Further information can be obtained from the Charities Commission.

It must be noted that any monies raised in the name of a particular charity must go there. If another worthwhile cause emerges while fundraising is going on, a separate fundraising programme must be adopted. Funds must not be diversified unless it has been stated from the outset that monies raised will be divided between two or more charities. Furthermore, be they individuals or groups, fundraisers must abide by the rules and regulations of the parent charity. The charity has an obligation to respect public opinion and avoid causing offence, both through its own work and that of groups aiming to assist them.

Many schools have become involved with raffles and lotteries following the success of the National Lottery. However, I am constantly amazed at the ignorance that exists about the law in this respect. Talk to the local council or to the local gaming board officer. For clarification, so far as charity law is concerned, lotteries are classified in three ways:

- Small lotteries. This classification refers to raffles that are incidental to the main attraction, such as at school fetes, bazaars, etc. Expenses covering the cost of raffle tickets and the cost of prizes up to £50 are allowed, but the remaining proceeds must go to the charity and not to private gain. In many cases these raffles can be conducted utilising cloakroom tickets. Cash prizes are not permitted and refunds on ticket sales cannot be made. The sale and issue of tickets and announcement of results must take place during the main event.

- Private lotteries. This refers to where tickets are sold only to members of a specific group such as a parents' association or football club. The tickets should be printed bearing the price and name and address of the promoter. The lottery should not be advertised except on the premises of the charity or their promoter. Expenses are taken into consideration, but otherwise all proceeds must go to the charity or to the provision of prizes.

- Public lotteries. These, or society lotteries as they are sometimes called, can only be organised by a registered charity or some other organisation that fulfils certain public criteria.

As long as these rules are adhered to, small and private lotteries can be conducted without seeking permission from the local district authority. However, public lotteries are the domain of the parent charity only. Please note that raffle tickets should not be sold by, or to, persons under sixteen years of age.

Competitions and gaming

These are regulated by the Gaming Act 1968 and the Lotteries and Amusements Act 1976. The purpose of both these Acts is to prohibit large-scale gaming activities on premises that are not licenced or registered for that purpose. Of course, these include schools, although the *St Trinians* films depicted a slightly different situation. There are relaxations in the law if the entertainment is promoted for purposes other than private gain. Activities such as bingo, whist drives and tombolas will usually fall within these exemptions provided all the proceeds (minus expenses) are devoted to the charity they are supporting. If a school is offering money as a prize, or expecting large numbers of people to take part in the gaming activity, enquiries should be made at the local magistrates' court as to whether or not the school should apply for a gaming licence.

The law and events
When organising events, be the school a registered charity or not, the organisers must be aware of their legal and financial obligations to members of the public who lend their support. They should think in terms of their safety and well-being, but also bear in mind the risk to themselves or their project if everything around them should collapse – and that's a very polite way of putting it. It's a worrying prospect but one that can be reduced if the relevant licences, insurance and safety procedures are taken into account.

Public liability insurance
This type of insurance covers the usual range of accidents that can occur to members of the public when they are invited to attend most types of event. It broadly refers to personal injury and property damage. So if at a charity cricket match the ball is cast out into oblivion and stops only at the windscreen of a visitor's Volvo, the costs incurred are covered. Similarly, should a member of the public trip over a tent rope and break a leg, your group is covered against any claim for damages which may ensue. Insurance of this kind is a worthwhile undertaking, as any settlements you may have to make, should an individual decide to sue, can run into thousands of pounds. For this reason, take care not to under-insure the event. The bigger the event, the larger the insurance undertaking should be. For a fete or sporting event you should be thinking in terms of no less than £500,000, and more if there are big numbers of people involved. Ask an independent insurance advisor for the best quotations available.

Theft

A separate liability to consider is the possibility of theft. You can insure against theft or loss of money, cheques, etc. on the day and at the location of your event. This will usually extend to the premises from which you operate and the homes of those involved in the fundraising. If you are hiring or borrowing equipment such as a marquee, check the insurance cover here. While a firm will usually have its own insurance covering lending and other uses of equipment, private owners acting from their own goodwill may not be covered. In this case, as organisers, you should take on the responsibility of insuring the specific item(s) of equipment.

Special events insurance

Some events are not covered by public liability insurance. These include some shows and exhibitions. A special events insurance cover may be necessary if, for example, you are expecting to loan more valuable items than fetes and sports events usually entail. I refer to exhibitions of art, antiques or specific craft or collectors fairs where valuable items may be on display. Again, check with an independent insurance advisor. Such provisions may incur an extra premium.

Fire

Public premises and certainly school buildings available for hire or functions will already operate safety regulations. These should be studied carefully and adhered to throughout the event. If you have any doubts whatsoever, for example regarding any limitation of numbers in a particular venue, enlist the support and advice of a local fire prevention officer, based at fire stations throughout the country.

Licences

Once you have planned safety procedures and insurance cover, the other legal consideration is the possibility that you may need certain licences to cover local authority restrictions on staging a public event. Outlined below are relevant licences you should consider. Further information can be obtained from your local district authority. Local authorities vary quite considerably in their interpretation and enforcing of the law, and I advise you seek clarification before proceeding.

- Entertainment licence. If you plan to charge an entrance fee, you should apply for a public entertainment licence. The local authority will require a month's notice of the event and it can issue yearly and occasional licences. There will be a fee, its value will depend on the type of licence (yearly or occasional) you apply for and the number of people you expect to attend.

- Liquor licence. If alcohol is sold at your event at any time, you are required to obtain a licence from your local magistrates court. In most cases, a representative will have to attend court for this purpose. Under no circumstances should alcohol be sold by, or to, people under the age of eighteen.

- Music licence. You should contact the Performing Rights Society if you intend to perform already published music. This body will usually waive their royalties claim if the cause can be shown in any way to the relief of human suffering. Whether or not educational fundraising is covered by this is obviously open to debate.

When noise can be a nuisance
If you are holding an event which could be noisy, involving loud music, rival teams, and so on, it's worth referring to your local environmental health department. They can give you guidelines on what levels of disruption are acceptable for the kind of event you are planning.

Trading

An important aspect in the context of charities is the trading one. Basically a charity cannot trade unless it is within the primary purpose of the charity. What this means is that if the school conducts trading on an educational basis it is all right. An example would be in the field of summer schools. Summer schools aimed at the further education of children would be considered as within the primary purpose of the charity and, hence, not be trading. However, if the school were to think in terms of courses aimed at adult education, it could be argued that these were not within the primary purpose and would hence constitute trading. The way to proceed is for the charity to set up a charity trading company. In this way, all income can be steered via the company and any profit after deduction of costs can be Gift Aided across to the parent charity each financial year, thus avoiding serious tax involvement, such as corporation tax on profits. This is a perfectly acceptable method of achieving a business within the context of a charitable organisation and that is how the high street charity shops operate. For advice on these matters, contact your solicitor or talk to either:

- The Institute of Charity Fundraising Managers, Market Towers, 1 Nine Elms Lane, London SW8 5NQ. Tel: 0207 627 3436; or

- The Institute of Development Professionals in Education, PO Box 102, Manchester M14 6XE. Tel: 0161 434 1847 Email: info@idpe.org.uk Website: www.idpe.org.uk.

Most legal considerations can be satisfied by completing a few forms and by spending time researching these areas at the beginning of your preparations. The trick is to confront all these considerations right at the beginning, so that you needn't worry later when more practical considerations are demanding your attention. Most fundraising will require nowhere near all the criteria I have presented.

Tax incentives

The Chancellor, in his April 2000 Budget, made some significant changes to the tax position regarding charities. With the abolition of any limit on Gift Aid claims and the ability to donate stocks and shares to a charity, schools can benefit considerably from acquiring charitable status. Though the old Deed of Covenant, much favoured by educational establishments, was also abolished, there is no reason why the process of regular giving cannot be encouraged with annual Gift Aid claims on donated money. Please note that any existing Deeds of Covenant signed before 6 April 2000 will continue to operate until they expire, with the charity claiming tax relief as previously. From this date, all tax relief will be by Gift Aid. It is a relatively simple and low-cost operation to set up charitable status and advice can be obtained from the school's legal advisors. It should be pointed out that there is some political threat to schools having charitable status and a close watch should be kept on this aspect. Once charitable status is achieved, tax-effective giving comes into play.

It is possible to give to charities directly from a bank account. Charities usually opt either for direct debit or standing orders. Some may use both methods. Most donors prefer standing orders, possibly as they believe that the decision to either change or stop payments is more in their own hands. For this reason, many schools do not use the direct debit method.

Direct debit payments are made through the bank on a monthly, quarterly, six monthly or annual basis. There is an agreement set up between the bank, the donor and the chosen charity. A direct debit allows the charity to draw a specific amount from an account at the times agreed. The amount can be altered by reaching a new agreement and the donor informing the bank that the charity can now claim the new amount. To cancel a direct debit, the donor must inform the charity that he or she no longer wishes them to draw from their account. A direct debit form must be completed and signed by the donor.

A standing order agreement is just between the donor and the bank. The donor instructs the bank to pay their chosen charity a given amount at specified intervals: monthly, quarterly, six monthly or annually. This gives the charity less control of their income and they may not even know where the donations are coming from. The donations can often be stopped without the charity being informed, the donor needing only to write to the bank. A standing order form or letter of instruction must be completed and signed by the donor.

Regular giving is the most beneficial way of contributing to the charitable funds of the school. The process is extremely simple. Any amount may be pledged, no sum is too small or too great. It is important that the donor chooses an amount that is appropriate to his or her circumstances and commitments. Changes in any of these can always lead to changes in the pledged amount. The donor may pay monthly, quarterly or annually and may select the period over which they intend to contribute. A normal pledge to give regularly will be for a period of four years, as with the old Deeds of Covenant, but please note that a pledge given for seven years, the normal lifetime of a child through GCSE and A-levels, will increase the amount contributed to the charity (including the tax recovered) by 75%. For UK taxpayers, a Gift Aid declaration will enable the charity to recover almost 30% in reclaimed tax in addition to the original donation.

Examples of the value of regular giving to a charity over a number of years
(based on income tax at 22%)

Net monthly amount Pledged	Net yearly amount Pledged	Total amount received Over 4 years	Total amount received Over 7 years
£10	£120	£615	£1,011
£15	£180	£923	£1,615
£20	£240	£1,231	£2,154
£25	£300	£1,538	£2,692
£30	£360	£1,846	£3,231

(Pledges for regular gifts can be for any amount, smaller or larger than these examples)

Other ways of giving include one-off gifts rather than a long-term commitment to regular giving. If the donor is a UK taxpayer, the charity will help make a Gift Aid declaration, enabling it to claim back almost 30% more than the donation in reclaimed tax to add to the gift. No sum is too small. Gifts can also be accepted from companies under the Gift Aid scheme. Gifts should be gross payments, the company being then able to claim tax relief in their tax computation. Great care should be taken when dealing with companies that no significant advantage be gained by the company from the donation. This is termed a 'consideration' by the Inland Revenue and will not have the benefit of Gift Aid. The definition of what is significant is limited to purely an acknowledgement (less than 5% of the total value of the donation) such as on a building, piece of equipment or book or role of honour. There are some cases where large fines have been invoked both on the charity and the company for claiming tax relief where a significant consideration has been involved. For further information on Gift Aid tax relief, you can obtain the leaflet *IR113 – Gift Aid* from your local tax office.

Examples of the value of Gift Aid including the tax recovery
(based on income tax at 22%)

Net amount given to fund	Gross amount received by fund
£100	£128
£500	£641
£1,000	£1,282
£2,000	£2,564
£3,000	£3,846
£5,000	£6,410

Stocks and shares can now be contributed to the charity. Further details are again available from the local tax office.

Higher rate taxpayers have to be treated somewhat differently as the charity is only able to claim back tax at the standard rate. This means that if the donor is a higher rate taxpayer, the donor will be able to claim back the difference between the rate he or she pays and the standard rate contributed to the charitable fund.

Legacies and bequests offer an opportunity for tax relief and this will discussed separately in another section of this book.

Charities Aid Foundation (CAF) is an organisation with which donors may have an account where they can deposit an amount. The CAF will reclaim the tax and add it to the account, effectively giving them around 30% more to donate. They may either have vouchers, which can be used as cheques, or a CAF card, which can be used as a credit card. It is important to remember that the tax has already been claimed by CAF, so it is not up to the individual charity to do this.

Payroll giving is a method by which the donor has a scheme at work where a donation to the charity is made before he or she actually receives the pay. The charity receives the full amount before tax, so does not need to reclaim the tax on that donation.

An unspecified pledge is the situation whereby the supporter promises to send some money within a specified time – usually two weeks – but is unwilling to state an amount.

All the above methods can add significantly to the value of a donation, and the potential donor can be encouraged by the fact that some of the tax paid does not end up in the hands of the Inland Revenue. With due respect to the Inland Revenue, this approach most often leads to donors having an enormous amount of self satisfaction.

An example of a donor support form covering all eventualities

.... School

Please complete in BLOCK CAPITALS and return in the pre-paid envelope

A. Your details
   Title .... Full Name ....
   Address
   ....
   ....
   Postcode ....
   Telephone No. ....
   Email ....

B. Form of contribution
   1. Regular giving: please complete the standing order below
   2. One off gift: I enclose a donation of £ ....
   Please make cheques payable to .... If you wish to make a donation by credit card, please tick here .... and return this form. We will contact you to obtain your credit card details.
   3. Transfer of shares: approximate value £ ....
   If you are donating shares, please tick here .... and we will send you the necessary forms
   4. Legacy pledge: I have made a bequest ....
   I am considering making a bequest ....
   Please send me copy of your legacy booklet ....

Standing order form
   To the manager (name and address of your bank)
   ....
   ....
   Account no .... Sort code ....
   Please pay £ .... monthly/quarterly/annually (delete as appropriate)
   For a period of four/seven/ten years (delete as appropriate)
   Starting on .... / .... / .... (date)
   To .... Fund .... Bank Address ....
   ....
   ....
   (sort code ....)

C. Please sign and date
   Signed .... Date .... / .... / ....
   Please treat my donation and all future donations as Gift Aid – see guidance notes below.

   Guidance notes
   We can reclaim tax on all gifts made under the Gift Aid scheme which means that every £10 you donate is worth £12.80 to the school.
   1. You can cancel this declaration at any time by notifying the school.
   2. You must pay an amount of income tax and/or capital gains tax at least equal to the tax the school reclaims on your donation in the tax year (currently 28p for each £1 you give).
   3. If in future your circumstances change and you no longer pay tax on your income and capital gains equal to the tax the school reclaims, you can cancel your declaration (see note 1).
   4. If you pay tax at the higher rate you can claim further tax relief in your self-assessment tax return.
   5. If you are unsure whether your donations qualify for Gift Aid, contact the school or ask your local tax office for leaflet IR113 Gift Aid.
   6. Please notify the school if you change your name or address. .... is a registered charity no ....

Chapter two

The role of development

The first steps

THERE IS little doubt that the education sector is about to undergo a major cultural change and, in some ways, follow other sectors in adopting new approaches to the funding of both capital projects and the general costs of running the establishment. A good example of another such sector may be seen in our hospitals, many of which now have their own appeals departments following the initial success of the Great Ormond Street Children's Hospital Appeal. Many will be aware of the situation, within the education field, in the USA and, to some extent, within the higher education units in the UK where fundraising to alumni and parents plays a major role. The universities have been extremely successful in raising millions of pounds. Initial steps have already been taken by a number of independent schools in setting up what are normally termed development divisions. But there is no reason why both Foundation,

Voluntary Aided and LEA schools should not follow their lead, particularly with the present government's statements on educational funding, and their encouragement for partnerships with the business community.

One obvious difference between independent and state schools is the lack of funds initially to seed development plans. By a realisation of the potential income generation that can arise from partnerships with local businesses, an income stream can be created that can go on to fund the other development plans of a more long-term nature.

Before any positive move is taken towards professional fundraising, great care must be taken in addressing the sensitivities of other fundraising initiatives that, in most cases, are already in place within the school family. Many parents' associations already hold smaller scale events, but are sensitive to the school's need to take a more professional approach. Nevertheless, it must be stated that the two can work very closely together and, in fact, involve very different markets. Provided consultation occurs at all times there need be no problems in this area. Similarly, the word consultation is equally important regarding the teaching staff, many of whom will find difficulty in accepting the changes in the school's approach.

For example, the school may choose to go down the line of the utilisation of its facilities for commercial gain. Many teachers regard their equipment and teaching aids with a degree of possessiveness and could be most obstructive to any external usage. However, if they are fully involved and their departments may be seen to benefit from such activities, most difficulties can easily be overcome.

A very serious consideration concerns the roles of the headteacher and governors of the school. The head must always be seen as a figurehead of any fundraising activity. His or her encouragement and participation is vital to the success of long-term plans. Similarly, the governors must be seen as being actively involved. Sadly, many members of the public become governors of a school as a recognition of social standing rather similar to being awarded a CBE, OBE or MBE. This is by no means true for all governors as many have been extremely hard working in support of the school. It must be made clear at the onset that the contacts and acquaintances of the governors are key people and the introductions they can create can give rise to major gifts.

The first step in fundraising is to come to an agreement on the allocation of resources. The only way to be successful is to create a dedicated permanent atmosphere of ongoing development with a reliable, accessible computer relationship database. Many schools have approached fundraising with a series of one-off appeals, perhaps every seven years, with no continuity or record keeping. The whole process should be ongoing. Particularly important is the concept of follow-up with regular updates and newsletters.

Many schools are reluctant to take the first step because of the lack of funds necessary to pay a fundraiser, or to buy the initial computers and office equipment. There is obviously a cost involvement in producing literature that can be sent to ex-pupils encouraging the idea of leaving a bequest to the school. But, a willingness to produce such literature can realise enormous benefits. There are examples of bequests of millions of pounds specifically left to the old school that, without much imagination, will be seen to easily pay the several hundred pounds initially involved in the preparation of literature.

The staffing of a development office

The education sector is unique. What charitable organisation has so many dedicated and warm supporters on hand just waiting to be asked for money? Having spent many years within an organisation that is constantly competing with other charitable concerns for the favours of the general public, it is refreshing to be a part of a profession where ex-pupils, parents and staff have one aim in view and obviously would not support other schools. We are in a fortunate sector that can exchange information and discuss successes and our few not-so-successful forays into the fundraising world.

Various options are available on the type and quality of personnel that are equipped and available to become fundraisers. It is not the role of a soon-to-retire teacher in the last two or three years before retirement. Fundraising is a professional occupation and must be done properly with the incumbent staff well aware of legal, historical and academic aspects and also with the ability to communicate and, most importantly, not afraid to ask outright for money. There is no doubt that many members of the teaching profession are quite capable of doing this. But training courses and visits to other schools with established development offices are crucial to success. A teacher may be one option to consider; others include a parent or ex-pupil.

A look at parents' professions may well yield an individual already working in the charity field and experienced in the art (or should it be science?) of asking for money.

If finances permit, an external appointment may be considered. There has been a rapid growth in the number of people doing this sort of work and there are plenty of available people. Many schools have considered recruiting from either the marketing or charitable fields with varying degrees of success. Care must be taken as to where to advertise – national, local or specific appointment publications. Consultants are available who will advise, short list and interview recruitment as required. This will be discussed in more detail later.

Salaries vary considerably with the type of school, and the scope and extent of the job description. Many schools expect their development staff to take on all the marketing aspects of the school. Others think the fundraising and marketing roles should be kept well apart. Both disciplines require the same basic principles. The portrayal of the school to prospective parents is very similar to the sale of the school to prospective donors. A range of salary from £15,000 to £85,000 can be found. Again, financial constraints control support staffing. With modern word-processor packages and a good volunteer base, it is possible to run a one man show initially until things really hot up, and constant thank-you letters and newsletter support fill the postbag, leaving no time for innovative ideas.

Care should be taken in the selection of an appropriate candidate from written applications alone. Unlike many professions, fundraising has only recently begun to adopt standards and professional qualifications. The Institute of Charity Fundraising Managers (ICFM) is attempting to set down aspects of moral and ethical practice, and a member of this body will be well aware of key issues. The Institute of Development Professionals in Education (IDPE) has been set up to oversee the profession as many now see it.

A school must also consider the contract of the new appointment very carefully. There must be a get-out clause, after about six months, for the rare but unfortunate complete disaster. On the other hand, it does take time to build relationships. You will have a good idea of the potential after about two years. Sadly, a number of schools have sacked their fundraiser after only six months because a deluge of money has not come in straight away. Please do not expect money to start coming in right at the start. If running costs are covered over the first two years, major income will be realised in the fourth and fifth years – statistics show this.

There has been much discussion within the charity sector recently at what are reasonable ratios of income to expenditure and some of these arguments are equally applicable to the education sector. Some schools have decided on a commission basis but be careful to put a ceiling on this. Most professional fundraisers are against working on a commission basis. There is a great danger of creating a smash-and-grab aspect that can seriously damage long-term relationships, which are so crucial to long-term support. Many a school fundraiser would spend several happy years in Barbados following a successful legacy campaign on a commission basis.

A relationship database

Within every school's family are individuals prepared to support the school who are just waiting to be asked. A lot of them do not, perhaps, recognise the need and should be constantly updated on progress and planned developments. In many cases this support may not be purely financial but may consist of gifts in kind. Unless every bit of information about parents, relatives, pupils and ex-pupils is at your fingertips, the potential cannot be realised. This is why the relationship database is such an important tool to the school fundraiser.

How many schools are there whose data about ex-pupils is either stored in dust-covered boxes in the basement somewhere, or hidden away in the memory banks of the long-serving teacher with an amazing recall of past students? I am reminded of an event I attended several years ago when I was asked to talk at a Rotary Club luncheon. Present was my ex-English teacher of more years ago than I care to remember.

"Ah, Poppitt," he said. "The class of '57," and proceeded to list every other boy in the class with an update of where they were and their life history to date. Many school share such an individual. Such a person is, of course, invaluable. But modern computer software does give us the ability to store this information and make it readily available at any time.

So, what is a relationship database? There is really no limit to the amount of information on an individual that can be obtained. During a recent trip to New York to attend a meeting of the National Association of Independent Schools, one experienced fundraising speaker, in response to a question, outlined the sort of information he stored on a given ex-pupil. He knew every detail about the school career including which sports team the pupil played for and what his non-academic interests were. Details such as "Did he collect stamps or play tiddlywinks?" were readily available.

He had details of all the pupil's relatives and what their jobs were, and knew full details of the individual's various occupations, the value of his property, the number of bank accounts and stocks and shares that he had and all about his current hobbies and interests. All this information was also readily available about all the parents; not just the name and address and contact telephone number that is usually the case.

Armed with such information, the fundraiser is able to classify the potential donor as a possible $2 million, $1 million or $100,000, and simply goes and asks. This will not always work in this country, but there is no doubt that knowing a pupil's uncle is a director of a local football club or a school supplier is a great help in knowing how to target.

To be able to approach a potential donor with a portfolio of his or her life history immediately gives the asker an advantage. I remember visiting an old boy at his beautiful home in Surrey where the initial reaction was not even to let me into the house. However, it quickly emerged from the conversation that I knew he had toured Europe with a particular eccentric Latin teacher and the conversation soon got to shared experiences and the recounting of many stories. He became a very generous donor to the school during the following years.

Modern software also allows us to target people by postcode or years at school. This is invaluable when attempting to network alumni and initiate reunion events at school or in other locales. A local ex-pupil can be identified and relied on to liaise with local hotels or university premises when contemplating a reunion. Experience has shown how important current undergraduates can be to such events as they are immediately seen as ambassadors of the school. The older ex-pupils love the opportunity of comparing their days to more modern ones. It is also extremely important that the database is kept clean, i.e. up to date. There is nothing worse than an individual receiving several copies of literature or it being sent to the wrong address, or even a recently widowed lady receiving a newsletter addressed to the deceased.

Interestingly, many schools keep in touch with widows or widowers of ex-pupils. They may like to continue to receive information about the school after their partner's death. It may seem mercenary but there are examples of widow's supporting their late husband's school. Modern software can check for duplicates and prevent the likely friction from such an eventuality. As the database grows it is increasingly important that one individual is given the responsibility either full time or on a part time basis, hence saving any problems of lack of continuity.

There is a tremendous number of options available for the purchase of database software and care should be taken before opting for a particular system. Do not be afraid to ask for a demonstration of the package and certainly ask for and contact other users of the system. By far the best way of judging a system is to talk to other individuals who use the system the way you want to. Many schools have their own expert IT specialist who may be able to design a system for you.

Database software suppliers

There are a number of suppliers with a lot of experience in the field, including:

Blackbaud Europe Ltd – The Raiser's Edge, The Claremont Centre, 39 Durham St, Glasgow Tel: 0141 427 7939

Capstone Systems – Ready Riter, 48 Woodpond Avenue, Hockley, Essex Tel: 01702 207742

Care Management Systems – DonorFlex, Patrick House, Lakeside, 180 Lifford Lane, Kings Norton, Birmingham Tel: 0121 458 7887

Df Consulting Ltd, 22 Grove Road, Newbury, Berkshire RG14 1UH Tel: 01635 33862

Westwood Forster Ltd – ALMS, 13 – 27 Brunswick Place, London N1 6DX Tel: 0207 251 4890

Fastfile Ltd – Mailkit, Ashley Green, Belmesthorpe, Stamford, Lincolnshire PE9 4JQ Tel: 01780 480010

FunderFinder, 65 Raglan Road, Leeds LS2 9DZ Tel: 0113 243 3008

SPSS (UK) Ltd, 1st Floor, St Andrews House, West Street, Woking, Surrey Tel: 01483 719200

Mercator Computer Systems Ltd – Snap, 5 Mead Court, Thornbury, Bristol BS12 2UW Tel: 01454 281211

New Generation Consultancy – AppealMASTER, Park IT Centre, Coryton, Okehampton EX20 4PG Tel: 01566 783371

Stak Computer Systems plc – MIDAS, 4 Badminton Court, Station Road. Yate, Bristol BS17 5HZ Tel: 01454 325258

Systems Partnership, 300 Hither Green Lane, London SE13 6TS Tel: 0208 687 3858

Tourmaline Computing Services, "The Answer", 14 Tower Street, Heathfield, East Sussex TN21 8PB Tel: 01892 853503

For advice from software experts in the development field there are consultants to contact who specialise in this aspect. The ICFM or the IDPE can supply lists.

Building alumni relationships – an American experience

On my first day in the position of director of development at Bolton School, I sat and perused the published list of members of the Old Boltonians Association. As an old boy myself I was particularly keen to know of the whereabouts of my contemporaries. But as a fundraiser I was interested in the distribution of successful ex-pupils all over the world. It soon became obvious that there was a large cohort in North America, many of whom had been extremely successful.

This, I surmised, could well have been the result of the 'brain drain' prevalent in the sixties and seventies when many young professionals, particularly British scientists, were tempted across the Atlantic by the promise of high salaries and splendid living conditions. Many of them stayed, brought up families, and had extremely successful careers. However, in a country almost obsessed with fundraising and alumni development (they term it advancement) I guessed, in many of them, there would still be strong feelings of nostalgia for their old school.

I believe that the building of long-term relationships is crucial to long-term support in terms of schools fundraising. There is an increasing amount of evidence supporting ideas that carefully nurtured alumni will help educational establishments again and again, leading to the ultimate and final big gift in the form of a legacy. This appears to be being realised more regularly in the education sector as schools concentrate on a long term development programme rather than one-off appeals on a smash-and-grab basis.

My work at Bolton concentrated on the relationship building aspects. By creating liaisons among old boys and girls in individual cities, we were able to set up local reunions all over the country. Cities such as Bristol,

London, Edinburgh, and areas such as Yorkshire and Cumbria, now have regular dinners with an increasing number of ex-pupils attending. It seemed the next logical step to think in terms of doing the same sort of thing in North America with some 50–60 names and addresses already on the database.

Perusal of past correspondence immediately brought to the fore a certain old boy, now living in South Carolina. Colin's letters to school had obviously indicated a very strong bonding, which he considered mostly responsible for his ultimate position of professor of urology at South Carolina University. Another key player in what was to come was the former school captain in 1959/60, a chap I looked up to with great affection even as a young first year student in those days. Now the marketing manager for Rank Xerox and an extremely successful businessman, Len also considered his education at school in Bolton crucial to his ultimate success. Both these individuals became key players in the reunion and were ideal people to be nominated as American residents representing the school in terms of the British Schools and Universities Foundation (BSUF).

The BSUF has been approved by the United States Tax Department as a charitable organisation, contributions to which are tax deductible. The American charitable tax laws differ greatly from British law. Indeed, there is a positive tax advantage to individuals donating to charitable organisations. However, these tax advantages do not exist if taxpayers in the USA want to support overseas charities. I was privileged, on the morning of the subsequent reunion in New York, to have breakfast with Scott Bushey, the President of the BSUF and we, together with my headteacher, who had accompanied me, had a fascinating discussion on the role of the BSUF.

It is really important that the BSUF is not seen as a conduit, but it does offer the facility for British schools to help themselves reach their US constituency and provides a way for US taxpayers to make tax-deductible gifts. The main requirement, as indicated above, is for a US resident to act as representative for the school or college. Further information in the UK can be obtained from Mrs Sheila Wiltshire OBE, 6 Windmill Hill, Hampstead, London NW3 6RU. Our school captain, Len, following his splendid support of Bolton School via the BSUF, has now accepted a position on the board of the Foundation.

The preliminary plans for organising the dinner relied on the willingness of alumni to travel what were, for many of them, quite long distances, and the establishment of a local liaison individual who could help finalise details with the venue. The first step was to contact as many American residents as possible and determine if they would be able to travel and, if so, where their preferred destination would be. Limited by rationale and locality of such an individual who would act as liaison, we offered a choice of New York, San Francisco, Toronto or Florida. Over forty replies came back with New York the most popular. Many other suggestions were received, with a feeling that the east coast dwellers were not keen to go right over to the west and vice versa.

Atlanta was a popular choice, with its amazing airport facilities. But after due consideration, New York was chosen with a date of 2 June 1998. This coincided with the presence in New York of our distinguished old boy – Lord Robert Haslam of Bolton, who kindly agreed to come along with his wife.

The venue was to be the Harvard Club on West 44th Street, mainly because Len had attended Cambridge University reunions there and was able to make the initial contacts. It was at about this time, six months before the event, that I really began to realise the significance of electronic mail. Without it, I actually doubt if we could have had such a successful event. By utilising this, Colin and Len were able to persuade a good number to attend.

With my flight and hotel booked, we managed to persuade the headteacher to come along as well. We were also aware of two recent leavers who were on English Speaking Scholarships in New York State. One of these happened to be an excellent pianist and the other a recent school captain who had benefited from an assisted place. As the main fundraising objective was to raise funds to attempt to finance bursaries to replace the assisted places scheme and maintain the key role of the school, an ideal programme for the evening began to take shape. Eventually 37 people sat down to dinner in the Harvard Club and a little bit of Bolton was created in the heart of New York that evening. The atmosphere was magnificent with diners constantly causing chaos among the poor waiters by swapping tables to discuss shared experiences and memories.

It was interesting to note that those present thought the atmosphere far superior to university reunions they had attended in the US. The sad part was in the farewells, which for so many came fairly early as long distances had to be covered that night. By 10.30pm all was still and quiet. I tidied away the memorabilia samples and school information displays, feeling delighted by the success of the evening, with a firm commitment from many of those who attended that it would be the first of many.

Financially, the event was an enormous success with gifts of over $120,000 secured and the promises of legacy commitments from several who attended. I would say to any school with records of ex-pupils in the US that this sort of event is well worth considering. I had even thought, if I could not get enough of our own alumni to attend, that it may even be worth combining with a couple of other schools of a similar nature to hold a joint reunion. After all, we are all trying to raise money from our own alumni to support our individual schools and are not in competition for our target supporters. I think there may well be an opportunity for joint events if there is a fear of very low numbers.

It was clearly stated to me during the evening that, if we didn't ask for money at some time, we would not be considered to be doing our job. This is in contrast to this country where I have found that there can be conflict if an old pupils' reunion is seen purely as a fundraising event.

Legacies

"Raising from the dead" or alternatively "Pennies from heaven"

It only seems right to give some space to a more detailed appraisal of legacies.

Have you made a will? Most of us do not want to face this situation, but the reality is that only about 40% of the population have. The rest face the very real situation that their estates can revert to the state on their death. Statistics are wonderful things but there is no doubt that, to charities in general, legacies represent almost 70% of their income, with very little effort and administrative burden. In any such consideration for schools it is extremely advantageous, but not essential, that there is a registered charity associated with some aspect of the school.

Our tax laws do offer us a last chance to have a swipe at the taxman by denying him income when we make a charitable bequest. Statistics again tell us that people who leave a charitable bequest actually live longer; surely the most persuasive of reasons. However beware, because recent figures also tell us that the majority of people die within four years of making a will. Other figures obtained recently have shown that there were 25,236 charitable bequests in a year and that 1,013 had a value greater than £500K.

Some current average legacy values

Cause area	Pecuniary	Residuary
Services/marine	£1,670	£15,936
Aged welfare	£690	£11,962
Overseas aid	£3,290	£17,939
Environmental	£2,660	£43,559
Education	£2,500	£17,932
Mentally disabled	£2,600	£16,652
Arts	£10,000	£32,500

Just a couple of examples show us that RNLI received £38.4 million and the Cancer Research Campaign received £39.3 million, from legacies, in 1995. Sadly from the education point of view, only 1.8% of charitable moneys comes our way. (Figures provided by Smee & Ford.)

With a background in the charitable sector, one of my first aims, in working with any school, is to investigate the potential of legacy income. In approaching this subject the main object is to point out to alumni how much we remember our schooldays as a groundwork for life and to encourage a thought of a bequest when contemplating death. The message is obviously not quite as blunt as this as I am very much aware of the sensitivities of the subject. The ideal way of presenting the subject is to prepare literature specifically about *The Will to Give*.

I have been successful in achieving this for several schools at no cost thanks to the help of local solicitors who have sponsored the booklet. This is not difficult and relies on tracing alumni in the legal profession who may be prepared to help on a philanthropic basis and see it as a way of supporting the school, or by a sales technique utilising the financial potential of probate. Every year there is a 'Make a Will Week' in late March affording an ideal opportunity to promote the subject.

I believe that it is important in preparing the literature to cover information about the subject of legacies in detail and only, after all considerations have been covered, to address the possibility of a bequest to the school. This would include the following:

Why make a will?
The answer is, above all, to protect your loved ones. Caring is what you do all your life and a will means that you can continue to care after your death. This protection is not just financial – you will also safeguard the peace of mind of your loved ones because if you die without making a will, the law decides how your possessions will be divided. Other relatives may have a claim on property that you had intended to pass to your partner or immediate family. Another possibility is that a widow may have to sell the family home because her children are awarded a share of its value. Guard against such eventualities – make a will.

It is imperative that children are provided for, especially if they are young and still dependent. If both parents die together, a guardian will be needed to look after them. In your will, you can appoint someone to take on this role. In the case of adult children, leaving a will could save family wrangling and a possibility of legal costs over who receives what.

Children can be provided for by setting up a trust in your will. This can have tax advantages. Your will must state who the trust is to benefit, what it will hold, the names of trustees and what powers they will have. A solicitor will advise further. There may be personal possessions such as books or jewellery that you would like friends to have. Any promises you make to them will be worthless unless such wishes are included in a will.

Remember, if you leave no will and have no relatives, everything you own could go the state.

Types of legacy
Naturally the first consideration in making a will is to take care of family and friends. Once they are provided for, consideration can be given to the inclusion of a legacy to a charity. Not only can a legacy reduce inheritance tax liability, it is also a wonderful opportunity to help others. There are several methods by which it can be done.

- Residual legacies. Many people choose to help charities by bequeathing the residue of their estate – that is the sum that is left after all other legacies and costs have been paid. This type of legacy is especially beneficial as the gain to organisations such as individual schools can be considerable.

- Special bequests. A specific sum of money or piece of property is left to the charity, but it is important to remember that inflation can seriously reduce the value of the bequest. To avoid this, a solicitor could index-link the bequest to the retail price index from the date of the will.

- Life interest. This is a way of providing lifetime security for a loved one and benefiting another person or organisation (your favourite charity, for example). By giving someone a life interest in your property, you can ensure that when that person dies, the property passes on to the person or organisation named in the will. A solicitor can advise on this.

- Leaving a legacy to charity. All gifts to charity are free of tax. By making such a gift, the estate can be brought below the inheritance tax threshold, which, at the time of writing is £242.000. No tax will be payable. For example, if your estate is worth £248,000 net, i.e. £6,000 above the tax threshold of £242,000, some £2,400 (40%) would be payable in inheritance tax. If you left £6,000 to a charity, the value of your taxable estate would be reduced to £242,000 and no inheritance tax would be payable. You would have put £6,000 towards a good cause, yet the tax savings mean it would have cost your estate only £3,600. The inheritance tax threshold rises each year and is linked to inflation. If there is doubt, consult your solicitor or accountant for the relevant figures.

Isn't making a will complex and costly?
In each case, probably not as much as you would think. It is important to follow these steps:

- Decide who you want to benefit. Before you start to make a will, be clear in your mind about this. Do you want your spouse or partner to have all, or almost all, your property and possessions? Do you want to protect your children? What about friends or other members of your family? Would you like to support any charities?

- Choosing a solicitor. It is important to select one who deals regularly with wills. You may have a family solicitor or a friend may be able to recommend someone. You could ask a number of solicitors and compare their charges. This aspect can be utilised to stress the sponsor's role in the preparation of literature, with due praise and recommendations as to the excellence of their service provision.

- Go prepared. It is important to have an idea of assets to hand when the solicitor is approached.

- Appoint an executor. This is the person appointed by the will maker to ensure that all wishes, as detailed in the will, are carried out. It may be wise to appoint two executors in case one is unable to act for you. An executor may be a member of the family or a close friend, and there is no reason why an executor should not be a beneficiary of the will. Alternatively, a professional adviser such as a solicitor, bank manager or accountant can be approached to act as an executor, but this will incur a fee that will be deducted from the value of what is left.

- Have the will witnessed. Once the will is drawn up and agreed, it needs to be signed and witnessed to make it legally binding. Two witnesses are needed and it must be signed in each other's presence. The witnesses and their spouses must not be beneficiaries of the will.

- Keep it in a safe place. The will should be entrusted to a solicitor or bank manager for safekeeping or kept in a safe place where someone trustworthy knows where to find it after death.

- Be wary of home-made wills. In making a will it is always better to use a professional adviser. Home-made wills can cause problems. The slightest mistake, even in names and address, can invalidate the will.

Why update a will?
Because a will that is out of date may be little better than no will at all. Throughout life there will be changes likely to have a direct bearing on a will. Marriage, divorce and remarriage; births or deaths in the family; a change in fortune for better or worse; or a change in who should benefit; are all potential factors that may change details of the will.

A marriage invalidates an existing will so, to protect the partner, a will must be made. A divorce means the former spouse will no longer benefit from the will. If a provision is to be made for the ex-husband or wife, a new will must be made. If there is just a separation and the spouse is mentioned in the will, he or she will benefit from the legacy, unless the will is changed, however long the separation has lasted. A new partner with whom the will maker is living, but has not married, will have no claim on the estate unless he or she is specifically named in the will. Remember, too, that the value of assets may change significantly.

If only minor changes are needed, these can be made by adding a codicil. This is a simple instruction added to an existing will. A codicil still needs to be properly drawn up and witnessed but is an excellent way of adding new legacies, such as bequests to schools.

The legacy literature can also contain the opportunity for future benefactors to let you know of their intentions and also full details of the correct wording necessary for the accurate distribution of the estate. It is also useful to have a glossary of terms used when making a will.

Does it work?
Having discussed the value of a positive legacy promotional policy for schools, it is only fair to give some examples. There are examples of schools and colleges receiving enormous bequests without even asking for them. A boarding school in the north of England recently received over £4 million from a single old boy who died leaving his entire estate to his old school. My own geography teacher left a sizeable bequest to Bolton School. I believe the success of the venture has been confirmed by the number of solicitors who have contacted me regarding the wishes of their clients. For example, a recent letter was received as follows:

```
Dear Sirs

We have been handed your booklet 'The Will
to Give' by a former pupil of Bolton School
who wishes to leave a substantial sum of
money in a designated trust fund in order
to finance a bursary or bursaries at the
School, on the basis that this would assist
families with financial difficulties to have
their gifted children educated at Bolton
School . . . and the school's solicitors could
look at it before the will is signed.
```

Any development programme needs to secure the long-term future support for the school and I remain convinced of the importance of a legacy approach to educational fundraising. I have no reason to doubt that such an approach will mirror trends in charitable giving. The potential of a codicil in support of a school can be sold as an attractive proposition as we get older and come to appreciate the importance of the education we received in our formative years. How often do we think that our school is where it all began, and we would not be in our present position in life were it not for the education we received? A legacy offers a small but significant way of repaying our thanks for this.

Trusts and foundations

There are approximately 3,100 grant-awarding trusts and fellowships listed in relevant publications, most of which are very specific in their chosen areas of support. Unless the correct approach is very carefully researched, you would be wasting considerable time and money in applying to many of these where you don't stand the slightest chance of eliciting support. Sadly, this is the case with the majority of applications and trusts becoming increasingly frustrated by the reams of applications that are completely outside their terms of reference.

To be successful in your application mostly requires a matter of elimination based on information from available literature. But, it has to be said, most successful applications have an element of luck. How fortunate it would be to know that the chairman of the trustees is a former pupil of your school. There is little doubt, as with corporate giving, that the old boy network can be most useful, and knowing someone who is a trustee can make life a lot easier. Once you have identified relevant grant-making bodies, why not circulate the names of the trustees to your governors? They may have met them or 'know a man who has'.

To give you some idea of the scale of money involved, grant-making trusts give £1 billion to charities each year. This is one of the major advantages in charitable status for your school, as discussed earlier, as most trusts of this nature stipulate this requirement. More than half of this enormous amount is given by 27 of the largest trusts.

Recently, the role of the National Lottery has become recognised by the education sector. There are a few schools who have been successful in Lottery bids to support their development. However, this is a very specialised area and in all successful applications has involved a major community partnership. Just to give you an idea, such a partnership will require 42 hours a week community involvement in the joint project. I do not profess to be an expert in this field and can only advise very careful research with your local council and consultation with experts in the field before you embark on any application of this sort. It is worth pointing out that the New Opportunities Fund does offer routes to substantial funding in the education sector.

Along similar lines, our involvement with the European Community also opens up certain opportunities for funding. The relatively new Leonardo and Socrates grants give seed funding to schools keen on entering into a partnership with other European schools. The British Council and reference books can help and advise you on the way forward. I have heard it said that if you go down the right corridor and knock on the right door in Europe, you can gain access to funds in support of any major project. If you know who it is, why not approach your local Member of the European Parliament. They may be keen to help if only to identify themselves to the local community.

Identifying suitable trusts can be made easier by consulting two major publications both of which will be available at your local library. They are:

1. *The Directory of Grant Making Trusts* (published by the Charity Aid Foundation);

2. *A Guide to Major Trusts* (published by the Directory of Social Change).

Both organisations also produce literature specific to educational trusts and there are CDs available, constantly updated. Many charities employ individuals specifically to work on this aspect. Information about local regional trusts, which are often the best bet for schools, can be obtained from your local Charity Information Bureau. Another source of potential grant making trusts can be the local solicitors who may have records of money placed in trust through their services. With regard to geographical location, some trusts are very specific indeed. One school discovered a bequest local to a particular borough that was specifically for the support of education of a child resident in that borough. The school was successful in obtaining £35,000.

Trusts that may support you can be identified either by geographical location within a specified beneficial area, as above, or by the relevant charitable field. Education is obviously a relevant field but others cannot be ruled out. Welfare can often include matters relevant to school life and many schools with a religious base can often benefit from trusts with a religious policy. There are many examples of schools benefiting from trusts set up for specific Anglican, Jewish or Roman Catholic educational teaching.

Over the last few years while working in the charity sector, I have been fortunate enough to meet several trust administrators. Conversations about their professional frustrations have enabled me to identify some important aspects regarding applications for funds from these, and similar, organisations. The following points may seem obvious but it is amazing how many applications make major errors that don't put your wonderful cause in a very good light. You must be aware of the following:

1. Doing your homework and not wasting time.

2. The correspondent should always be addressed by name and not as Sir/Madam.

3. Avoid a photocopied letter and be personal.

4. Get spelling and grammar right.

5. Keep it short – one side of A4 – if they want more, they will ask for it.

6. Only include a financial report if required – again, if they want it, they will ask for it.

7. Ask for a precise sum of money, which must be within the published budget that the trust has available.

8. Inform the trust if you are applying to others – they often talk among themselves.

9. Include a letter of appreciation of the school by a well-known ex-pupil.

10. Make sure that your particular project is not excluded by trust policy.

11. Don't be emotional.

12. Don't imply that you can't survive without their help.

13. Invite a visit and extend hospitality.

14. Don't duplicate the application.

15. Don't re-apply for at least three years.

16. Use the 'old boy' network if you can.

17. Telephone initially, unless specifically requested not to, to see if you fit the bill.

18. Include a stamped addressed envelope.

There is a lot of evidence that patience and perseverance often reap benefits. A recent exercise in one school saw 250 trust applications yield only three positive responses but income of £39,000. An interesting case study is Giggleswick School. This is based in a somewhat remote part of Yorkshire. Grant making trusts proved a significant source of income where there is little local industry and opportunity for business involvement. They advise against sending loads of letters in a scattergun approach. Indeed, the school asked distinguished local people to write to trusts on its behalf and was pleasantly surprised by the response. They had expected an income in the region of £20,000 but finished up with around £100,000.

The telephone in fundraising for schools

In the modern technological age, the use of the telephone probably represents one of the innovations that our great grandparents would have found the most difficult to accept. However, while being a superb communication tool it, unfortunately, has become a much abused system with sales techniques for timeshare and double glazing systems interfering with our lives just as we put the evening meal on the table. Any discussion of the use of the telephone in schools funding must take these factors into consideration and great care must be taken that the school is not tarnished with using methods that cause so much upset. By taking the right steps and employing the correct techniques, the telephone can yield enormous benefits

Charities have spent a lot of time and money on research into the best ways of persuading people to give them money. There is little doubt that face to face fundraising comes first on the list of successful approaches, but this is closely followed by highly profitable appeals by telephone, leaving direct mail in a rather poor third place. The prime fact is that people give to people and less to pieces of paper. Potential donors find it very difficult to say "no" when asked if they would be prepared to give on the telephone. It will be interesting to see how the new technology of the Internet, particularly Email, is utilised by the fundraiser. I think the telephone will continue to be successful by the very nature of the one to one communication. It also provides flexibility and enables small tests to be tried refining the 'ask' gradually according to the response received.

My use of the 'ask' does not purely refer to the solicitation of funds. The importance of a strong relationship database has been stressed many times in numerous publications and is now universally recommended to charities throughout the voluntary sector. To acquire all the information so important to development in the education sector, the telephone offers us an ideal instrument. Information on the career of alumni, both at school and since leaving, on the database can yield data not only of interest to the fundraiser but to the careers department and staff responsible for finding work experience and placements. Telephone campaigns can provide that situation when ex-pupils will love to swap stories of their school days, particularly with recent leavers. The universities have been pursuing these methods for years. I regularly receive calls from undergraduates in the faculty of the university at which I graduated. In the USA, if graduates don't get telephoned, they complain.

A major decision in approaching telephone fundraising is a choice of agency or an in-house operation. Some schools, such as Lancaster Royal Grammar School and Sherborne School, have been successful in using an agency, and have raised considerable sums of money. There are undoubtable skills in telephone management and I recommend the use of a consultancy at least at the training stage. I decided to use our own alumni at Bolton School to telephone other alumni, initially over a period of three weeks, but used the knowledge and skills of MDB Fonebase, Consultants, to train the callers. This was essential to the success of the venture and gave me a fascinating insight into the psychology of donor acquisition. Many consultants then offer hands-on management of the campaign, but I was keen to maintain a personal presence and to save the obvious costs of such an involvement. The consultants were extremely good and were at the end of a telephone line if I needed help.

It was decided to conduct a random exercise by selecting 750 old boys of the school on the database for whom we had telephone numbers. There is a CD-ROM available at low cost which will supply telephone numbers of all BT directory listed subscribers. Unfortunately, there is little one can do with ex-directory individuals unless they have already given you their number. We then wrote a letter to each of the 750 saying that we would like to telephone within the first three weeks of July to discuss future developments at the school. The recipient could Email, telephone or write if they did not want to be contacted. We had been told by the consultant that we should expect about 10% to contact us a this stage to say "don't ring". In fact exactly 76 did do this. What was totally unexpected that these 76 who did not want to be contacted actually enclosed cheques to the value of over £5,000. Contact was also made with a widow and sister to two ex-pupils, now living in the highlands of Scotland, who, following a visit from myself, made a substantial donation and the promise of a legacy.

Recruitment of callers was an interesting task. We decided to look for some recent leavers with suitable personalities. I needed one particular manager of the operation and approached a recently graduated Oxford University boy for this. He had asked the school for some administrative experience during the summer before taking up full time employment and was an excellent choice as team leader. Four other ex-pupils were recruited, one in his second year of a medical degree and three of that year's leavers prior to them going to university. I was present throughout the venture.

After seeking advice on legal and other considerations, the calls were made between 6.30pm and 9.00pm Monday to Thursday and 2.00pm and 4.30pm Sunday afternoon. In some cases, people had just put the tea on the table or were enthralled with the current *Coronation Street* situation. In these cases it was asked when it would be convenient to ring back. There were no serious problems encountered and I actually got to talk to a couple of old boys who I had not spoken to for 35 years. Many of the conversations became fascinating as young and old swapped reminiscences of school days, and there was obvious delight from many at the opportunity to do this. There was a script provided by the consultant but, in most cases, this became somewhat irrelevant.

Eventually, as indicated in the script, the 'ask' took place and received, as might be expected, a varied response. To some it created that one to one environment that reminded them that they had been prepared to give and stimulated the pledge. Others who had not considered giving were so impressed with the youngsters that they talked to that they pledged support. A vital contribution to the success of the venture was the teamwork and bonding created by the callers. Every success was shared with the others and any caller having a bad spell was immediately consoled and encouraged by the success of his friends. Overall it was a fascinating experience that yielded wonderful support.

For every call made a record sheet was filled in with full details. In every pledge case, a letter was sent the very next day fully confirming the details. If nothing had materialised within three weeks, a further letter was followed by another telephone call. This ensured that over 90% of the original pledges matured into regular giving as Deeds of Covenant, Gift Aided donations or credit card pledges.

The costings were as follows. Expenditure covered the consultants, the callers' remuneration @ £4.50 an hour and the hire of equipment. The latter included headphone sets to help the callers write and talk and refer to the record sheets. The total cost of the operation did not exceed £6,500. The income, including tax claimable from tax advantageous giving, was over £40,000. A random trial operation had laid the foundation for future fundraising efforts. Future projects would not require the training input as I now had those training skills. We then began to realise the significance of the telephone by using it for donor upgrades, lapsed renewals and covenant renewals, with enormous success.

In conclusion, I recommend schools to seriously consider a telephone campaign. With little financial outlay and the commitment of several individuals, substantial funds can be raised and links can be personalised leading to the long-term relationship building among alumni that is essential to ensure financial support for the school well into the future.

The role of consultants in fundraising

Many of the ideas and strategies included in this book have relied on the school having sufficient resources to implement a fundraising programme. Some schools are fortunate in having funds or staff time available for the initial investment that can yield long term results. However, the usual situation is to have no funds to employ a development director and therefore rely on voluntary help from a member of the PA, or to direct a teacher to do development for several periods a week. Both these approaches rarely work and create an unfortunate view that fundraising won't work at this school. Although it is difficult to get this theory accepted, fundraising is a profession and the skills required for success need to be accessed. To be a professional fundraiser is not easy, as many people have been brought up with the impression that it is an amateur role. This is certainly the case in the charity sector where voluntary committees are responsible for a large proportion of charitable income. For this reason an organisation known as **IDPE** (Institute of Development Professionals in Education) has been created as a non profit making body to establish the professional nature of development aspects. Further information is available from PO Box 102, Manchester M14 6XE. This body has produced its own Code of Practice on professional behaviour and standards.

To a school about to embark on a major project relying on the raising of money, several options of consultants in the field are available. As Harris Rosenberg states in his *Handbook for School Fundraising*, there are basically two types, i.e. project or process consultancy. Project consultancy looks at a distinct job whereas process consultancy will enable a school to continue the process after the consultant has finished the work. In other words, the former usually implies some hands on involvement or long-term advice on a regular basis, whereas the latter would most likely involve a feasibility study leading to an appointment of suitable personnel to oversee the project.

Consultants' fees vary considerably and can be within a range of £350.00 to £1,000.00 a day, depending on the experience and skills of the organisation or individual. They can also vary from one-man operations of a general nature to large organisations, with individuals specialising in certain areas such as alumni development or legacy promotion. There is often a certain attempt by a school employing consultants to instigate a commission basis with a percentage being paid on the successful completion of a fundraising project. This is not encouraged by many consultants who do not like the smash and grab approach, which can seriously damage long term relationships with the school, either of a business or individual nature.

When considering consultancy, always talk to the organisation on site. Many consultants will come to see you on a no obligation basis. As with employing members of any profession, there is an ideal opportunity to get the consultants to present a strategic approach to your project. You can thus compare and contrast different organisations and methodology and decide how you would wish to proceed. It is wise to ask for references and then you can talk to other schools that have gone down this track.

It is very important to decide exactly what you want from the consultant and this can be directly related to your existing resources. Many consultants offer distance management or an advisory service on a one or two days a month basis. Some are prepared to put in an individual on site to do all the work.

Any contract with a consultant must, according to the Charities Act 1992, be the subject of a Professional Fundraiser's Agreement, stating clearly the nature of the relationship and the duration and terms of reference, together with the remuneration details. It must also clearly state that the professional fundraiser must declare his relationship with the parent body on any approach for financial, or any other type of, support, and terms relating to early termination and any variation. A sample agreement as approved by legal advisors can be found at the end of this chapter.
Further details are available from the IDPE (above) or

the Institute of Charity Fundraising Managers, Market Towers, 1 Nine Elms Lane, London SW8 5NQ.

As in many professions, it is the most successful who decide to turn their hands to consultancy so track records are usually very good. To employ a consultant for one or several days a month can utilise many years experience in the field to the advantage of your school, at a small percentage of the total cost and potential problems that are associated with a full time appointment. It has been said that fundraisers are basically salesmen and sell themselves better than anything else. Sadly, only one in three succeed in fundraising. Monitoring and judging success can be difficult, and any project will need some basic research and data accumulation before money starts to come in. It is vital that the consultant is not expected to do everything. He or she will need administrative support so as not to waste valuable and expensive time on routine aspects. Utilising consultants can minimise risk in this area and prevent long term problems associated with ineffective staff and potential redundancy.

Professional fundraiser's agreement

This agreement made on the .... 20 ....

between

(1) The .... School, ... ("the School")
Registered Charity Number

and

(2) The Consultant. of ....
("the Professional Fundraiser")

Witnesses as follows:

1. Introduction
1.1 The School is an institution established for the education of children.

1.2 The School requires ongoing consultancy with the aim of assessing the provision of funds both from philanthropic and commercial partnerships in support of development projects ("the Project").

1.3 By an Agreement of even date herewith and made between the School (1) and the Professional Fundraiser (2) the School authorised the Consultant to make all necessary enquiries leading to consultancy as in 1.2.

2. Method of Operation
2.1 The Professional Fundraiser will comply in all respects with the provision of The Charities Act 1992 as amended.

2.2 The copyright for all purposes in all artwork, copy and any other work capable of being subject to copyright and produced or created by the Professional Fundraiser shall vest in the Professional Fundraiser. For the avoidance of doubt the Professional Fundraiser shall only be entitled to use such names and logos as are supplied by the School solely in relation to the Project and any materials supplied by the School will be returned to it within 28 days of the completion of the project. The provisions of the Clause shall subsist without limit of time notwithstanding the provisions of Clause 3.1 below.

2.3 The Professional Fundraiser shall ensure that any solicitation is accompanied by the necessary statement as required by the Charities Act 1992 and prior to the commencement of the solicitation shall produce to the School all marketing and sales material for approval which will deem to be approved by the School unless any written objections are received by the Professional Fundraiser within 14 days of the supply of the material to the School.

3. Period of Agreement
3.1 This Agreement will expire after a period of twelve months from the date of the Agreement.

3.2 Discussion as to further Consultancy involvement will ensue at this time.

3.3 The Professional Fundraiser will devote .... days per calendar month to working with the School, due notice being agreed and stated one month in advance as to the days involved each month.

4. Termination

4.1 The Agreement may be varied by mutual agreement.

4.2 Either party may have the option of terminating this Agreement without notice in the event of either party being in breach of any of the terms hereof.

5. Financial Provisions

5.1 The Professional Fundraiser will request remuneration in terms of £......... per day for all work involved in consultancy. Invoices will be submitted monthly with payment preferred within 30 days.

5.2 The Professional Fundraiser will request all reasonable travelling and overnight expenses be paid directly to its representative on standard School rates.

5.3 The Professional Fundraiser will not require any additional fees from the Charity unless agreed between the Charity and the Professional Fundraiser.

6. General

6.1 Neither party shall without the written consent of the other during or after the currency of the Agreement disclose any confidential information relating to the other which is acquired as a result of the Professional Fundraiser's involvement with the School PROVIDED ALWAYS that the Professional Fundraiser shall be at liberty to use as it thinks fit any general marketing intelligence in pursuance of the Agreement.

6.2 Whether or not this Agreement has been terminated, neither party will take legal proceedings for the enforcement of the terms of the Agreement or of any rights arising under it, without first having taken positive steps to resolve the matter by negotiation, mediation or other informal method of dispute resolution not involving publicity.

6.3 It is intended that this Agreement will be executed on the School's behalf by two properly authorised officers of the School.

6.4 Any notice to be served pursuant to this Agreement shall be served by recorded delivery in an envelope addressed to the other party at its last known address and such notice shall be deemed to have been received within four days of posting.

6.5 This agreement may not be amended by either party without the written consent of the other party.

6.6 This Agreement shall be governed by and construed in accordance with the laws of England.

THE SCHOOL FUNDRAISER

Signed .... on behalf of The .... School

Name ....

Date ....

Signed .... on behalf of The .... School

Name ....

Date ....

Signed .... on behalf of The Consultant.

Name...

Date ....

Chapter three

Imaginative event management

TO MANY, events involve a good deal of work with very little return. A well-managed event can be extremely profitable and have potential benefits in networking and relationship building in addition to actual income. In my former role at the Christie Hospital I was responsible for organising two extremely successful Tapathons (tap dancing marathons), which realised some £165,000 net profit. They were so successful that a further one was realised with Wayne Sleep in July 2000.

Many schools have well-structured parents' associations or committees of ex-pupils that represent a group of hard-working individuals prepared to help. For any type of event a small sub-committee representing all factions should be set up and tasks individually assigned. At any time a school can find an anniversary of some aspect to hang an event on. I have worked with schools who have celebrated not only the creation of the school, but also the anniversary of a new building, the introduction of co-education, or the retirement of a long serving staff member. Even schools without details of ex-pupils readily available have an opportunity to start networking, utilising the reunion as a focus to attract back ex-pupils. Records can then be accumulated and an opportunity to ask for support for the old school acted upon.

Many schools do not have suitable premises for such a prestigious event. In this case, think of local hotels or restaurants keen to work with the school and attract your school family as potential clients. The whole range of potential business partnerships discussed elsewhere in this book opens up.

The many opportunities of running different events are probably well known and include race-nights, car boot sales, fashion shows and promises auctions. There are many organisations keen to find premises to hold an event. At one school the local model railway society and the orchid society hold their events annually, which appeals to their own members as well as to parents and ex-pupils. A central point to organise a vintage or veteran car rally or a treasure hunt can be very popular. Many people will travel a fair distance (and pay a sizeable entrance fee) to visit a craft or antique fair. Valuation days, which many antique dealers will run, attract the rich and poor who would love to know their pot ducks are worth a fortune. Another popular type of fair involves dolls. The names of contacts can be found in the specialised magazines located in supermarkets and newsagents.

If it is thought that there may be limited attendance at such events why not consider working in partnership with a local charity? Provided both parties agree to the fine details, and a proper agreement is drawn up, an event can be marketed to both the school family and the database of the local charity, and both organisations can profit from a successful event.

Probably the easiest and most popular events hinge on the arts and sporting aspects of the school. Concerts, carol services, school plays and literature evenings can always be a source of income generation. Invited guests, such as local authors or musicians, can attract an interested audience. All the above also provide an opportunity to invite potential representatives of local business into the school to sample the excellence of the presentation. The standard of theatrical and musical performances in schools these days is far greater than in the past.

Despite the obvious attraction of the school sports fixtures there are many opportunities for other sporting events. Local celebrity teams, such as disc jockeys at the local radio station or representatives of the soap opera cast, can often be invited to take part in a cricket or football match. Many large football clubs have 'veterans' sides with well-known names who will always be glad of a game. Any such fixture will attract an audience and the presence of a celebrity will greatly enhance the numbers. Have a look at who is appearing at the local theatre and approach them for an hour of their time. Most of these celebrities also have agents and details can be found in the local public library. This source can provide the basis for the true and tested sporting dinner. A well-run dinner with a good MC, comedian and sporting personality, can raise £3,000 – £4,000 with auctions, raffles, stand-up bingo and 'bunnies'. The latter requires a flip of a coin while the participants place their hands on their 'head' or their 'tail'. All who are wrong sit down, and the game continues until one is left standing.

A little imagination and a small group of people can run

and enjoy a whole variety of events, which not only bring much needed extra income but also stimulate local people to recognise the school as a vibrant and active organisation, keen to work in the local community.

How to organise a summer fete

A popular event, practised in some form by all charities, and one that has the potential to raise funds for every school in the land, is the summer fair or fete. As we have all had experience of days spent picking our way through muddy fields, searching for the tombola stall, and taking home countless pots of jam (none of which were eaten), the impression many people have of events like these is that they are very simple to organise. This is not the case.

There are 101 things to remember from the start, and even more as the fateful day looms nearer. For this reason, the golden piece again is to plan ahead. A poorly attended and badly organised summer fete can be very miserable. If the planning strategy is organised, right from the start, an enjoyable and profitable event can be the result. The size of such an event should not put you off, as long as you take it step by step and avoid the temptation of taking cuts. A well known school in Edinburgh raises around £10,000 from an annual fete on one day in the summer.

Before you start
Among your committee members and prominent volunteers you should have a number of people who already have experience of helping at fetes, better still if they have direct experience of organising one. Agree on a suitable date. Does it clash with any major sporting event or local pageant? And so on. Always be certain that there will be access to the toilet and catering facilities.

Legal considerations
Always do these tasks first to avoid problems later.

The School Fundraiser

1. Consult your local council. Inform them of your intentions. They may have objections, or offer further advice on legal constraints pertaining to your area.

2. Inform the local police too. They will be concerned with the numbers of people expected to attend and the location of your event, as these elements could contribute to parking difficulties, obstruction, etc.

3. Apply for any licences you may require, particularly Entertainments, Liquor, Music, and Gaming (if applicable); consider noise levels.

4. Safety: Approach the British Red Cross Society or St John's Ambulance for assistance on the day. Please remember that these are both charities and a modest donation would be much appreciated. Co-operate with them fully. Provide them with a sheltered first aid post, close to the nearest exit (in case an ambulance needs access).

5. Consider the money you have available to fund necessary expenditure. If members of the committee and volunteers are dipping into their own pockets to pay for materials, etc. ensure that your treasurer or bursar is keeping detailed accounts of such deductions. Expenses should be returned to the volunteer, but accurate records are essential. Decide on the budget that you have available. You may already have several hundred pounds from previous fundraising events. Divide this money into reasonable estimations of how much food, stalls and chairs will cost if you need to hire them and try to keep to this budget.

Each stall will also need a float of money at the beginning of the day. Such projections of the initial expenditure will help you to arrive at a profit margin you can expect from the event. A big mistake people often make when pricing items to be sold on each stall is that the initial expenses are ignored. Remember, you are not in profit until all your expenses have been settled. Do not under price your refreshments, bric-a-brac, programmes or side shows. Consider how much the public will expect to pay for such items, not what you feel would be an irresistable bargain.

6. Start the publicity ball rolling. You'll need extra help from the beginning and lots of interest in the event.

7. Decide on the stalls, side-shows and games you want. Don't overcrowd the space you have available, but equally don't let the field appear too sparse. Put similar stalls alongside each other to create a natural flow to the buyer. Stalls selling savoury sausages and light snacks should be close to stalls selling sweet things – home-made sweets, jams and biscuits.

Stalls
You will find below some ideas for stalls. These can be used as they stand or adapted to suit particular interests.

- Tombola. An old favourite. Ask local shopkeepers or parents to donate prizes for this. Label each prize (such as soap-set, camera film, make-up bag, etc.) with a number from a book of cloakroom tickets. Then put the matching tickets (folded) into a revolving drum or similar container. Most Conservative, Labour or working men's clubs have such a drum and will lend it to you for the day. Fill the drum with other tickets that do not relate to a prize. Aim for a 1:5 ratio. If using different coloured books of tickets, ensure the colours are averaged out across the prizes.

- Books and records. A must for all enthusiasts – try to have sections divided throughout the stall. Unusual jazz records for example, or crime fiction, children's books, autobiography, fundraising books, etc. Price the books or records according to their condition and popularity.

- Baby stall. Offer home-knitted and crocheted garments for babies. Blankets, booties and bibs are also good sellers. Don't under price any of these items for sale. If they were for sale in leading children's wear outlets, the cost would be high, so gauge your prices accordingly.

- Arts and crafts. Canvass donations from evening classes at your local college. There are so many unusual and beautiful things that can be made by enthusiasts. Try to cater for lots of different tastes and colour schemes.

- Fashion. Second-hand clothes can be a real bargain to seasoned hunters. Try to have a selection of Victorian items, especially Victorian lace garments as these are always attractive to the romantic at heart. Include jewellery, but do ensure that any fastenings such as hinges, studs and brackets still work. This stall could also offer the opportunity of second-hand school uniform sales, as many children grow out of their uniforms long before the uniform wears out.

- Cakes. As a centrepiece attraction, why not ask a local bakery or private enthusiast to donate a beautifully decorated Christmas or birthday cake. You could raffle this or have a 'guess the weight of the cake' competition. Members of the public pay 25p for each guess they make. Have a steward at the table to take down precise estimations and the names and addresses of each competitor. The winner should be announced on the day. Please note, no two competitors are allowed to guess the same weight as there must be one overall winner.

- Food. Make this look as attractive as possible. Decorate with a clean tablecloth and perhaps posies of flowers. Offer jams, preserves, home-made sweets, wines, pickles, etc. Be very clear about how long the items for sale will keep. If they should be refrigerated, or if they can be frozen, say so. The Environmental Health Department operates very strict guidelines on this, but briefly, all foods should be prepared, stored and served in the very best hygienic conditions. I assume schools can apply the same rigid standards to this sort of event as they do to feeding the children.

- Refreshments. If you decide to locate this a little distance from the main arena, such as within the school buildings, signpost it clearly. A lot of money can be made from the simplest refreshments. Divide the responsibility for the different types of food offered between your volunteers. Have plenty of sandwiches available, scones with fresh cream and jam, little cakes and biscuits and hot tea, coffee, chocolate, etc. For cool items such as fruit juices, home-made ice-lollies and ice-cream, have the use of a freezer/fridge and lots of ice cubes. Offer paper plates, disposable knives, forks and spoons, as this will save on the washing up. Take such expenditure into consideration when pricing the refreshments. It is nice if you can have tables and chairs for people to sit down and relax.

- Plants. This could include dried flowers or posies of potpourri, as these are very popular now. Offer bedding plants (in season), cacti and houseplants. Again, price according to condition and original value.

- Bric-a-brac. For smaller items, little ornaments and other knick-knacks.

- White elephant stall. An extension of the bric-a-brac idea, but with larger items. Ensure that everything you sell is in good working order.

- Toys and games. For the children, so make it look as attractive as possible. If you're selling jigsaws and other games, do ensure all the pieces are together. Sellotape lids onto boxes to prevent any loss. Also think in terms of home-made toys and clothes for dolls.

- Good as new. Items here should be exactly that. Try not to present tarnished goods hoping people won't notice. They often do. Include last season's clothes and accessories for all the family.

- Wedding stall. For summer weddings offer pretty garters, posies, pretty white lace handkerchiefs and pillowcases, along with other similar items.

Side shows
These are the entertainment of the day. Old favourites such as Punch & Judy shows always attract a crowd of children – check your local press for names in your area, or failing that, your local library will have directories of entertainers.

Organisers of fairground rides and quad-bikes will often give you commission on monies taken on the day. Negotiate a price or rate of commission with them, but be sensitive to their constraints. Many children's entertainers earn their living from events such as yours and therefore may not be able to sizeably reduce their charge.

Some corporate bodies such as banks have their own bouncy castles, etc., so a few research telephone calls may yield a benevolent organisation, keen to advertise their benevolence by letting you use their equipment. There are many other possibilities for hiring, but be aware that you may have to book several months in advance as these are very popular – particularly in the summer months.

There are obviously many possibilities for side shows, but here are one or two ideas proven over the years to be very popular:

- Unroll the toilet roll. You will need: plastic sheeting, a distance marker, blackboard and chalk, toilet rolls, tape measure, pen, paper and clipboard. Contestants are invited to cast the toilet roll across the plastic sheeting, unravelling as it rolls. A measure is taken of the distance reached without it breaking. At the end of the afternoon, the winner is announced and presented with a prize. keep an account of names and distances scored, put the leading contenders on the blackboard. This will encourage and attract other contestants.

- Stop the candles. Make a large square sponge and layer it with thick icing. Then place into the icing as many candles as possible in tight rows. Contestants pay an amount to try and blow out as many candles as they can. A winner is announced at the end of the afternoon and presented with a prize. Be careful not to burn yourself or others when lighting the candles. When working out how many candles have been blown out, count the ones still alight and deduct them from the initial number placed on the cake.

- Fairground attractions. Side shows such as the 'wet sponge & stocks' contest, 'test your own strength', and other such games, can be hired for an event from fairground amusement operators. A willing teacher will be the centre of activity when the children in his or her class have an opportunity of throwing a wet sponge at him or her. Check the Yellow Pages for details. Do not include open gambling side events, other than the raffles and competitions already discussed, which are allowed under the rules of the Gaming and Lotteries Act. Gaming can only be undertaken in licenced premises.

- Throw the shuttlecock or wellington boot. Similar to the 'unroll the toilet roll' contest, contestants are invited to throw a shuttlecock or wellington boot as far as they can. They have two attempts and you should record the best one. The winner is presented with a prize at the end of the day.

Guessing games

As well as the tried and trusted 'Guess the weight of the cake' competition, you could also use this principle for other competitions. Canvass out the contest by mingling with the crowd. If the item is not too heavy, one person could carry the object, while another enlists names for entry.

As with other attractions, the following ideas will prove more profitable if a sponsor donates the prize. Thus, for the 'Guess the doll's name' game, a toy retailer or manufacturer could be approached and so on. Here are some ideas for you to consider. Don't use them all, the public will become irritated if they are constantly pestered by stewards.

- Guess the doll's name. The committee members each choose a name for the doll or teddy bear. They write their choice on a piece of paper, and place it in an envelope. The envelopes are shuffled and then all but one of them are destroyed. This ensures that not even the committee members know the chosen name. Contestants guess a name and fill in a form with their own name and address. These forms are then folded and put into a drum. At the end of the afternoon, the sealed envelope is opened and the author of the first correct name picked from the drum is the winner. When committee members are choosing names, don't be too obscure. You do want a winner. An alternative is to use scratch cards. These are now commercially available.

- Guess the number of sweets in a jar. Ask a local shopkeeper to give you an empty sweet jar and fill it with small sweets such as dolly mixtures. Use the same administrative format as above.

- Guess the number of embroidery stitches on a piece of fabric. Use a variety of stitches, in random patterns and sizes. Use the same administrative format as above.

- Guess the number of stitches in a knitted garment. As above, offer the garments as the prize.

- Guess the number of sequins on a dress. If you can, hire or borrow a ball gown used in ballroom dancing competitions. Display it indoors on a dressmaker's dummy. Don't allow it to be soiled. Pin a sign on the chest asking people not to touch the dress.

A Christmas bazaar

Apply the principles for a summer fete when planning the event. You'll need a large hall with enough room for the stalls and refreshments. The school dining hall is ideal, especially with the close proximity of kitchen facilities. Try to make the whole event as seasonal as you can. Decorate the interior of the room with bunting and presents (which can be raffled) around a Christmas tree. The food stall could sell Christmas puddings and biscuits in popular Christmas shapes, such as Christmas trees, bells, holly leaves, etc. On the cake stall you could raffle a Christmas cake, and do have lots of items for sale that would be attractive to the buyer as potential Christmas presents. Why not approach a major department store for a Christmas hamper, or alternatively make one up yourself? You could hold a competition to guess the value of the hamper, or simply raffle it.

A jumble sale

Many of the points below apply equally to the well used car boot sale, but be aware that the quality of both the goods and some of the so-called members of the public who frequent this type of event is not guaranteed.

The School Fundraiser

It is recommended that you plan this type of event well in advance. Rally volunteers to collect jumble for a couple of months before the day. You could prepare brief notices of the date and time of the jumble sale and the collection times too, and make sure all the parents and people living in the surrounding area receive them. The children themselves are often seen collecting jumble for scouting or guiding or school endeavours. If children are collecting jumble they should be in pairs and supervised by an adult. Approach the collections street by street, so the adults can keep an eye on children who should be discouraged from wandering off and collecting on their own. They will after all be knocking on the doors of strangers.

When collecting and advertising the sale, make sure the public are aware of the cause you are supporting. The venue, date and time of the sale should be publicised as often as possible. Make bright clearly laid out posters (ask the children to design these) and ask permission to display them in libraries, shop windows, on church notice boards, and in bingo halls, and be sure that the event is well publicised in school newsletters and notices to parents.

Divide the jumble into men's, women's and children's clothes and keep the best of these for a 'good as new' stall. Shoes should be on a stall of their own. So should books, bric-a-brac and (if applicable) collectors' items – this category can include rare books, medals, tins, toys, antiques, old photographs, etc. Label each stall clearly and have a refreshment area prominently signposted. Have someone on the door collecting a small admission charge from each entrant.

Even the best jumble sales have residual items unsold at the end of the day. There are second hand clothes dealers who will view the remaining items and offer a price to take them off your hands. It is unlikely to be high, but then the headache of disposing of unwanted jumble is solved. Be careful not to sell antique objects for a give-away price.

If you find something that is of high value, consider its origin. Elderly people, in their willingness to help, can quite innocently donate something of a much higher value than they could have imagined. If this happens, and you do know where the item came from, inform the original owner. They may decide to donate the object anyway or to make a separate donation in gratitude for your honesty.

Children and fundraising

Children make wonderful recruits to fundraising and the already suggested link to a local charity can greatly enhance their involvement. Children have an enthusiasm and energy which is rarely matched in adults. Their involvement in fundraising for a partner charity is also an excellent opportunity for them to learn about situations outside of their own. Fundraising events should offer an opportunity for the child to learn about the need to help others and to discover skills and resources in his or her own character. There are a number of ways you can do this, but also some considerations, many of which apply equally to the school day, to be aware of right from the start.

The most important element in involving children in voluntary work is to maintain their safety. Children should be supervised by at least one responsible adult at all times. They should not be allowed to wander off and collect jumble or seek raffle ticket buyers in private houses. Unless supervised, door knocking should be discouraged. In terms of physical safety, areas where there is insecure equipment, hot pans for cooking, electrical equipment, etc. should be out of bounds to younger children where possible. Similarly, children should not be encouraged to assist in the lifting of heavy equipment.

The biggest problem when involving children in fundraising activities is with holding their interest. As all teachers know children become very bored very quickly, and understandably so – a lot of organisational elements in fundraising are tedious. The best way to counteract boredom is to set a series of challenging tasks to be achieved. Give some responsibility to groups of children. One group could be responsible for decorating three or four of the tables at a summer fete, or, equally wrapping up the presents attractively for the tombola or raffle prizes. Another group could be asked to make models to sell or arrange, and man a stall of the event.

When choosing fundraising events directly aimed at children, try to be as imaginative as possible. Choose themes that will amuse and captivate them. Here are a few ideas of events aimed at children, and later suggestions of how to involve children in wider fundraising events.

Parties
Fundraising parties for children can be organised in two ways. You could hold a small house or garden party with lots of attractions and theme games and activities, or you could organise a field party, similar to a garden party, where scores of children are invited to attend. For larger, garden type parties, an entry fee is charged and side shows and amusements are included. Here are some ideas.

- Fancy dress competition. For best results this competition should be publicised several weeks before the event. Divide the judging into categories dependent on age, for example 3–6, 7–10, 11–14. If the party is close to Christmas or Easter, you could suggest this as a theme to the dress. Offer prizes in all categories and consider how much the child has contributed to the making of his or her costume. While parents should assist their child in making the costume, children who have spent hours over their outfit are often bitterly disappointed when they know another child has won who hasn't assisted in the making of their costume at all. Alternatively, you could have an

Easter bonnet parade. Here children are asked to make their own Easter bonnets. They can be pretty, scary, funny or have themes such as science fiction or cartoon characters.

- Miming to the record competition. As the title suggests, children are invited to mime to their favourite pop song. They could also dress up to look like a pop singer. There is a good chance that either a father or elder brother or sister of one of the children is an aspiring DJ. Spread the word and see who comes forward.

- Teddy bears' picnic. This is an opportunity to seek sponsorship for an event. Held by a wood or large park, invite children from the school to take part in the picnic with the teddy bears. However, first they have to find one. Have second-hand teddies (washed) hidden in the surrounding field or wood. Children should be accompanied by adults. You'll need to collect a number of teddies beforehand. Put out an appeal on local radio (they are always looking for community involvement) and invite the local press to come and photograph the event. Alternatively, each child could bring his or her own teddy bear. You could offer prizes for the best dressed teddy, most loved teddy, bravest teddy (for teddies without an eye or loose stitching).

- Children's pet competition. Have a reasonably sized area set aside as a pet arena, so that judges and the audience can comfortably view the pets on show. Approach a local vet to be the judge. The competition should be divided into several classes. Here are a few ideas:

    - Puppies – of all breeds;
    - Dogs – miniature adult;
    - Dogs – large adult;
    - Cats – all breeds;

- Rabbits – all breeds;
- Other pets, including hamsters, stick insects, mice, spiders or snakes.

The judge should be looking for evidence of good health of the pet, a well-maintained coat, bright personality and signs of obedience. This might prove slightly difficult in the stick insect class, but a little imagination can win the day. If possible ask the children to parade their animals around the arena. They will love this; their very own Crufts. Why not include a prize for the most mischievous pet? Charge an entrance fee and provide refreshments close by.

Sponsored events
Children respond very well to a direct challenge, but make the idea imaginative. They will be more determined to stick with it if the whole idea has triggered their imagination.

- A children's sponsored silence. Every teacher's dream. Encourage the children to gather as many sponsors as they can. On the day, assemble them into groups around tables and provide plenty of reading material. They can play board games, but must not speak – even if their opponent cheats.

- Sponsored swims. A few schools are fortunate in having their own pools. If not, approach the chairman of your local swimming club with this proposal. Safety is of paramount importance here. If you use local authority facilities, such as a swimming pool or sports centre, you will have to ask their permission. Always remember that many smart hotels have their own fitness centres and swimming pools and may be glad of the ensuing publicity from a school event. Volunteers should be sponsored on a distance or time basis. Ensure that the children do not over-exert themselves. They should be tired but not suffering from exhaustion. Discuss with the local instructors or your PE staff a time limit to be set on the event. After a couple of hours in the water, some children (depending on their swimming ability) will be very tired. For a sponsored event such as this don't have a winner. All the children can do in events like this is compete against themselves – the best form of competition anyway.

- Sponsored cycle ride. Approach a local cycling club or one of the professional organisations that organise this type of event. I know of a group who do an extremely well organised Manchester to Blackpool cycle ride annually and anyone can take part, for a fee, for any charitable body. If you decide to do-it-yourself, take sound advice on safety procedures. Consider the numbers you expect to take part. Plan your route carefully and, if necessary, inform the police of your intentions. Ensure that everyone has access to their own water bottles or provide refreshment points along the way where they can snatch cups of water. Some may have seen the professionals do it this way in the Tour de France.

- Knit-a-square. Each individual knits a six inch square. These are collected and made into one giant blanket or quilt cover, or a collection of cushion covers. You can raffle such items at a fair or bazaar. Similarly, each knitter could be sponsored for every square he or she produces.

Children in the kitchen. If you have a food or cake stall as part of your event, encourage children to contribute to this. They could make little cakes and biscuits to sell as tuck for charity at playtimes. I have very long lasting memories of selling home-made treacle toffee, made by my mother, on the school corridors at the age of ten, to raise money for a swimming pool for my primary school.

Meringues

Ingredients
2 eggs
113g (4oz) caster sugar

Method
1. Separate the egg yolks from the whites.
2. Whisk the whites briskly until they form stiff peaks.
3. Add 57g (2oz) caster sugar to the bowl and whisk again.
4. Now fold in the remaining 57g (2oz) with a metal spoon.
5. Spoon the mixture, in oval heaps, onto a baking tray covered by prepared grease-proof paper.
6. Let the meringues cook for 2–3 hours or until they are dry. Transfer to a clean surface and leave to cool.

These can be sold as light snacks as they are for children, or made into sandwiches with butter cream in the middle. Decorate with pieces of glazed fruit.

Chocolate cracklies

Ingredients
28g (1oz) sugar
28g (1oz) butter
28g (1oz) cocoa
1 tablespoon golden syrup
28g (1oz) cornflakes

Method
1. Melt the sugar, butter and cocoa in a medium sized pan, over a low heat. Add the syrup.
2. Remove from the flame and add the cornflakes.
3. Mix in the cornflakes well, then spoon small piles of the mixture onto a dish and leave to set. Serve as little cakes to have with tea or coffee. Present them in paper cases.

Peppermint creams

Ingredients
454g (1lb) icing sugar
1 egg white
juice of half a lemon
peppermint essence

Method
1. Sieve the icing sugar into a bowl. Combine with the egg white.
2. Knead the dough with your hands. It should be pliable. Add the lemon juice until it reaches this consistency.
3. Now add some peppermint essence – not too much though, up to a teaspoon is enough.
4. Cut into crazy shapes with a knife. Sell as sweets.

Sweet lemonade

Ingredients
lemons
lemonade
caster sugar
crushed ice

Method
1. Squeeze the juice from the lemons.
2. Put just enough lemon juice into a glass, so that is just covers the bottom.
3. Add a spoonful of icing sugar; the more you add, the sweeter the lemonade will taste.
4. Add crushed ice to the glass.
5. Fill with lemonade. Serve with a straw.

Knickerbocker glory

Ingredients
2 bananas
3 colours of jelly: green, yellow and red
ice cream
peaches – cut into segments
strawberries

Method
1. Make up jellies in the usual way.
2. Begin to load tall glasses in the following way: green jelly – ice-cream – peach segments – red jelly – strawberry – ice-cream, etc.
3. Top with ice-cream and slices of banana.

Here are a few basic recipes your children can adapt and improve upon.

Sporting events

Sporting events are excellent fundraisers. If they are organised and publicised effectively, they attract wide support and can be a very enjoyable way of inducing people to charity work. On three occasions I have been involved with massive charitable tap-dancing events with the late Roy Castle, Norman Wisdom and Wayne Sleep successively. There is no doubt that a total of over 12,000 people, over the three events, thoroughly enjoyed themselves and raised over £200,000 for charities. On a smaller scale, such events can be a steady and guaranteed way to raise money for schools.

The main source of revenue from such an event comes

from the monies raised by the number of people who sponsor you to succeed in the challenge you're taking on. And this is the key to a successful sporting endeavour. The activity you undertake must be a challenge. It must involve a commitment from you to try to achieve a goal that is outside your usual level of skill or interest. This does not mean that you should choose an activity that is totally beyond your reach. No-one expects you to jump off the edge of a cliff, clinging onto the rail of a hang-glider, unless you know exactly what you are doing.

When you are choosing the kind of sporting event you would like to organise, choose something you are already familiar with. If you are a member of a sports club or are involved with a school sports team, there will already be present in your group a knowledge of the rules and safety considerations necessary for a successful event. This is an excellent base from which to work, as experience can only add to the success.

When you prepare sponsor forms, ensure that the scope of the event is described in full. Sponsors should be certain of how much money they are committing themselves to. Divide the event in terms of laps, miles, goals, etc., and state clearly the limit you expect to reach to give some indication of the sums involved.

Consider the time you have available for planning the event. If its success is dependent on good weather, make sure you have reserved the area in good time and take care not to clash with regular school fixtures. Check other activities in the neighbourhood around the date you have planned; the summer months will be the first choice with other groups as well as your own. Consult an independent insurance advisor too, as you can, in certain circumstances, insure your event against bad weather. If, for example, your charity cricket match is completely rained off, you may be able to claim compensation from

the insurers for the monies lost due to the weather on the day.
Fitness
When planning the event, consider the level of fitness and skill needed to successfully complete the challenge. If training or coaching is likely to be needed, allow for this when deciding on the date of the event.

Dissuade volunteers from taking part if they have medical conditions likely to be worsened or aggravated by the event. You should be clear, from the start, about the distance or length of time the players will be committed to, so that no-one feels obliged to take on more than they can chew.

You should also consider whether to include children. They will usually have lower levels of stamina and endurance and these factors should be taken into account. The Sports Council can advise on the age limits you should employ for each type of event. You could divide the event into two competitions, one for adults and one for children. But, however you organise the event, have first aid facilities and water available along the route or near to the field.

Safety
When organising sports events, safety must be your paramount consideration. You should plan for the numbers you expect to take part in and watch the event. Consult St John's Ambulance, they may be able to attend your event and can give informed advice on safeguarding the health of everyone on the day.

At the event, you should have a first aid tent (or room) in a prominent position, manned by a qualified first aider; or, if your event takes place along a route, as in a walk, run or cycle trek, you should provide a vehicle with first aid equipment.

As a volunteer participant consider the precaution of

insuring both yourself and your event under special accidents insurance. Some injuries, such as a broken leg or collarbone, can mean absence from work for several months. Also, insuring against loss of earnings is a wise precaution if you taking part in an activity where you could be at risk.

Prizes

Having a trophy or prize to present to the winner of your event will increase the prestige and support. Trophies can be bought from any good sports shop. Ask the store manager if you can do a deal to keep the costs down. You could also approach a local company, perhaps a wholesaler or retailer, and ask them to donate a prize in exchange for free advertising (posters, programmes, etc.) on the day.

Judges

Where appropriate, without being too dogmatic, insist on fair play. Obvious examples of cheating or 'nobbling' the other side's best players can only reflect badly on the cause you are supporting. When appointing referees they should have a thorough knowledge of the game, and any amateur experience or accredited qualifications in the field.

Planning a charity sports event – some general points

1. Allow enough time for training and getting fit, etc. Is the event relevant to any particular season?

2. Consider the following legal requirements – some or all may apply to your event:
    a) Entertainments, Liquor, Music Licences.
    b) Are noise levels likely to be high? Consult your local authority.
    c) Will parked vehicles cause an obstruction? Consult your local traffic police.
    d) Will the necessary provisions be made so that any

food you intend to sell on the day has been prepared, stored and served in hygienic conditions?

3. Publicity. To increase interest, try to make aspects of your publicity relevant to the particular sport you have chosen. For example, you could approach a local professional football or cricket club for a signed shirt or football or cricket bat, to auction on the day, and this should be a prominent feature of your publicity. When approaching a well known sports personality to make a celebrity appearance at the event, don't be surprised if he is unwilling to join in with play. There may be a clause in his contract which forbids him to play in amateur competition in case of injury. If a popular celebrity is going to be there on the day, consider this when deciding the entrance charges to the event.

Field sports events – points to remember

1. To reduce the risk of injury, ensure that the playing area is a good distance from stalls, side shows and any other attractions you have included on the day.

2. Have a first aid tent or room, clearly signposted, close to where most injuries could occur. If you have the use of a tannoy system, announce the location of the first aid facilities at points throughout the day. A collection point for lost children could also be located near to the first aid tent.

3. Clamp down on fouling, incorrect and dangerous methods of play. In contact sports consider the importance of wearing safety gear. This is especially relevant if children are playing. If mixed teams of children and adults are included, make sure that differences in height, strength and fitness are considered, where relevant.

4. Have refreshments (particularly fluids) readily available near to the playing area.

5. If the weather turns inclement, stop play for a while. Injuries are more likely to occur on insecure, muddy ground.

Route sports

1. If the trek, run, cycle, etc, takes place along public highways, consult local authority and police departments.

2. When publicising the event, state clearly the route you are taking, so that people can support you along the way.

3. Have water and first aid officials at regular points. Also, if possible, have someone with a stopwatch and timesheets there to give information on the performance of competitors.

Other sporting ideas

- Sponsored fish-a-thon. Every sport can be turned into a fundraising event. If fishing is your hobby, why not hold a sponsored fish-a-thon? Approach a local fish farm to support you in your venture. The idea is to ask sponsors to offer an amount (e.g. £1.00) per fish caught. You could offer fish dishes and salads for sale and give a prize to the best angler.

- Slow bicycle race. Incorporate this challenge into a summer fete or fair. Each competitor lines up at the Start and, on the whistle, begins pedalling as slowly as he or she can. He or she mustn't fall off the bike or put his feet on the ground to steady their balance. The last one across the line wins.

- A golf tournament. Imperative for this venture is the support of a well-situated golf club. They should have good facilities and a well-maintained course. Alternatively, you could hold a smaller event on a pitch-and-putt course or croquet lawn; the same principles of organisation apply.

Approach celebrities and, if your event is big enough, even perhaps semi- or professional golfers.

The players are divided into teams of four, with an equal distribution of talent and experience in each golf team. Administration and standards for the course should be the responsibility of the club itself. The club may require payment for use of facilities, administration, etc.

Offer other attractions on the site too. The usual stalls and refreshments can be varied with sporting displays, mini auctions and autograph signings by celebrities, if possible. The success of an event such as this rests on wide publicity. If you do manage to attract celebrities or professional sportsmen, charge an entrance fee that reflects your coup.

For the more adventurous

Experience in fundraising and a knowledge of the chosen event is essential to bring success and subsequent rewards. There are consultants specialising in this field who will advise you. When embarking on larger-scale fundraising ventures remember:

1. Plan ahead – allowing plenty of time for training.
2. Seek any licences or permits required, well in advance.
3. Plan any safety procedures thoroughly and seek advice where necessary.
4. Enlist the aid of volunteers you know you can rely on.

For some of the sporting events mentioned below, the risk of personal injury is increased if proper advice and safety procedures are not pursued. Seek the advice of experts and accredited associations only. The financial returns to the charity or school you are supporting should be greater for such events, and this criteria should be a measure of the effort involved. There is also usually a higher initial cash lay-out to be made. Consult the headteacher and finance departments before embarking on a major event. They can offer constructive advice on financing and managing the event. Don't forget the advantages of partnerships with local charities on these types of events.

- Parachute jumps. An increasingly popular stunt for some fundraisers. The latest main competition appears to be bungee jumping. Centres where you can train and make the jump, under expert supervision can be found in most regions of Britain. The British Parachute Association (BPA) is the governing body that oversees the practices of the growing number of private companies set up to manage the sport. The BPA has a list of accredited centres throughout the country and it is advised that you make an initial enquiry with them.

On applying to a parachute centre, you will receive an application form detailing such information as the age, height and weight of each person taking part. I can remember striving to put on a little extra weight when one of my friends suggested we try this. The extra weight meant I was unable to participate – how sad. The company may require a deposit from you at this stage. Once your application form has been processed, it will be returned to you along with details of when and where the jump will take place, an official sponsor form and medical form. Most companies will already have insurance arrangements with a reputable insurance company, but you should check this before committing yourself to the jump.

Jumps generally take place over a weekend. A full day's training course is on the Saturday, and you jump on Sunday. The big money to be made here is through sponsorship. For this reason, allow at least a month to canvass as many sponsors as possible. Some charities specify that, should the jumper raise twice the cost of the jump and survive, he may withdraw his expenses from the proceeds.

- Abseiling. Although often featured as an event in itself, abseiling originated from the sport of rock-climbing as the second fastest route of descent. The British Mountaineering Council advises that abseiling should not be considered as a fundraiser unless the volunteer has sufficient experience to lessen the risk of injury.

Groups who do favour rock-climbing or abseiling as potential events should seek the advice of an accredited British mountain guide. Further details can be obtained from the British Mountaineering Council.

- Assault courses. For the very fit, the challenge of competing against others and an assault course could be the sort of challenge you're looking for. The army has assault courses throughout Britain, which are primarily used in training their personnel. The army will sometimes allow courses to be used for events in aid of charity. Contact your local army HQ for details of courses nearest to where you live. There are now several organisations that specialise in organising these and other events. While the majority of these are perfectly legitimate, a certain degree of care should be taken when employing these organisations and you need guarantees in writing of all the costs involved. Always check with the police or the ICFM for the authenticity of these groups.

- Water-skiing. The British Water-ski Federation overseas accredited club events throughout the country. Competitions can consist of three disciplines: jump; slalom; and tricks. If you are a member of a water-ski club already, such a competition could result in a sizeable return. Have sponsored events, collections on the day, with programmes and refreshments for sale.

Contact the British Water Ski Federation for further guidance.
- A prison break-out. A less arduous but equally competitive stunt for small groups is the prison break-out. Volunteers, suitably kitted out in fancy prison dress, are split into groups of three. They assemble at the nearest prison gates at 12.00pm Saturday afternoon. Each group has 24 hours to get as far away from the prison as they can, without spending any money. At 12.00pm on the Sunday, they should obtain a piece of evidence from their furthest location and then begin the journey home.

To prepare for this event, have sponsor forms printed. Ask people to sponsor you per mile or make a lump sum donation. Publicise the event in the usual way, and approach local travel firms for free return tickets to use on the day of the event. Airlines, coach firms and railway operatives have all been known to donate free travel to a good cause. And who knows how far you could get? Even Australia is only 22 hours away.

Some words of warning
When volunteers are travelling in such a free manner, there is a small degree of risk attached. When dividing your volunteers into groups. distribute male volunteers wisely. Young people under the age of eighteen should not take part unless closely supervised by adults at all times.

Theft/Insurance
You may need an up-to-date passport, and you should take with you some money for food and dinner. Safeguard any personal items in a money belt or secure pocket with fastening. Ask the advice of an independent insurance advisor as to whether extra insurance should be undertaken. Some countries do not operate a free health service and a broken leg can be very expensive.

Prepare a sheet of paper with the rules of the break-out clearly laid out. Distribute this to volunteers some time before the day of the event. Then, just before the teams depart on Saturday, announce the rules once more to reinforce safety procedures. For example, some of the rules could be: All groups must travel and return together as a complete group. No one should travel alone at any time. Although the event is a race and the pressure is on to win, do exercise clear judgement on your travels. If someone looks dodgy, trust your instincts and don't accept their help. Mobile phones are always useful, adding that little extra security.

The winners
The group that has returned with evidence of the furthest location wins the event. This evidence must be authentic and not a souvenir of a holiday three years ago. Encourage competitors to bring back items such as tickets and programmes bearing the date. This proves that they were there on the day. Everyone should report back by Monday evening at the latest. Announce the winners at a dinner dance or disco evening where each group can recall some of their experiences. One fundraising idea can stretch to two fundraising events. Present the winning group with a major trophy and remind all volunteers that if not already recovered, sponsor monies should be submitted by a set date.

- Dinner dances. If the school hall is not suitable, you will need to hire a hall that is large enough to hold the numbers of people you are expecting to attend. It should have tables and a dance floor.

Food
For a small- to medium-sized event, provide a buffet. You could contract out for this work, but catering yourself is another way of reducing costs and there will always be some parents willing to help. Divide the

responsibility of the food among your volunteers. Plan carefully so that there are even numbers of savoury dishes to match sweet ones. Ensure that all foods are prepared, stored and served hygienically. If it is not your trade, don't try anything too extravagant. Most people will enjoy simple dishes, presented attractively. The aim is to make a buffet meal tasty rather than adventurous.

Music
When approaching DJs for your evening, invite several quotes. Some DJs will attend for a nominal fee if the event is for charity. On the evening offer him or her refreshments and, if necessary, help with the loading and unloading of equipment.

Remember to confirm all bookings in writing. For the Winner's Dance of the prison break-out, put aside 45 minutes to an hour (no longer) for when the chairman asks a representative of each group to briefly describe their journey. Some of the experiences will be very funny and should make for an entertaining evening.

- Sporting dinner. A larger, more formal event involves inviting a well-known national sports personality or celebrity to give a speech after everyone has enjoyed a three-course meal. Many schools of all types are fortunate enough to have such a person among their alumni, a point which emphasises how important good records of ex-pupils are. As this is a more formal event, you must plan well in advance. If you decide, for any reason, to go out of school, negotiate with the hotel banqueting manager for a suitable price for the room and catering facilities.

When deciding on the sporting personality or celebrity you would like to attend, remember that giving a light-hearted, informed and interesting speech is not a skill all celebrities possess. In fact, some personalities will not inflict upon themselves such a burden. Most theatrical agents will know which of their celebrities are willing to attend such events, and you should approach agents first in this instance. There is a publication annually called *Artists and their Agents* (Offord Publications), which lists the agents and contacts for most well known celebrities. *Who's Who on Television* (published by ITV books) is another useful reference. There are some agents who will organise the whole event for you but again be sure of all the costs before signing any document. Any such individual should also be the subject of a Professional Fundraiser's Agreement, as discussed elsewhere in the context of consultants. Reference books of this nature are always available at your local library.

Once you have recruited the services of a well known personality, use their name to sell tickets. Negotiate a favourable price with a local printer (perhaps he or she could have a larger than usual advert on the tickets themselves), or tactfully enlist the support of your reprographics technician, and then allow time to be able to sell the tickets. To the reprographics technician constantly reproducing teaching material, the challenge of creating and producing an original design can be very rewarding to both parties.

When considering the price of tickets you have to consider the cost of staging the event, as it is likely to entail a high initial out-lay. The celebrity has to write and present his speech. This cost could run to several hundred pounds. I know of one or two renowned Rugby Union players who, never having been paid in their playing careers, fall back on after dinner speaking to enhance a normal wage. There may be the hotel, DJ or band, and printer to consider too. Not all of this outlay has to be met through ticket sales. Try to attract some degree of sponsorship from local businesses. Approach firms who already advertise through, or sponsor the sport you are referring to and, in particular, look to school suppliers. Raffles too can bring in a sizeable amount. If you can sell a selection of autographed authorised souvenirs in the lobby of the hotel, this will also increase your returns. The aim should be to make a profit. Ticket prices of over £20 may have to be considered.

The whole event is a balancing act: balancing the attraction of the evening and the personality you have attending; and the sizeable cost of holding the event. If planned well in advance and the celebrity or sports personality you have enlisted is likely to be popular, the financial returns on such an evening can be relatively high.

- Hot air ballooning. Hot air ballooning is increasing in popularity. And for the fundraiser, it is an imaginative and resourceful activity, which will attract wide interest and support. You should contact your nearest club and consult with them on the best way to incorporate the sport with your fundraising intentions. Many corporate bodies such as banks and building societies now have their own balloons and would like the publicity associated with the school or charity.

Ballooning could be part of a summer fete – as long as you have enough space available. Or you could offer the chance of a balloon ride as the main event of your day. Raffle tickets should be sold well in advance and the people selected should be briefed for their safety and comfort by the ballooning experts. Alternatively you could hold a 'Guess the distance' competition, where a hot air balloon is released into the air at a set time. Stewards at the release have stop-watches and after two hours the balloon is brought down. Members of the public are asked to predict the distance and direction the balloon has travelled in those two hours. The nearest correct answer wins a prize, which could be a balloon trip.

This relates closely to the idea of a balloon race with members of the public buying tickets which are then attached to helium filled small balloons. The ticket from the balloon travelling the furthest is the winner. You also need to offer a prize to the person who sends the recovered ticket back from the furthest point. Check all the legal requirements. It would be quite unnerving for an airline pilot to be confronted with a hundred balloons soon after take off.

A final word on event management

Organising fundraising events can be both fulfilling and a little hairy at times. The golden rule to remember is to plan as efficiently as possible right from the start. Have your own check-list where you can keep a record of where you're up to in completing the tasks you have personally taken on. If you are the chairperson of a committee, you should cast an eye over the other committee members' duties too. This is a delicate task in itself and one which should be approached with care. At all costs, avoid arguments. No-one can foresee every eventuality and some things are bound to be overlooked. But with goodwill, most events usually turn out to be a success.

Be realistic in choosing and planning your event. Satisfy any legal requirements first, including insurance. Always make safety the paramount consideration, and keep accurate financial records.

The only thing that remains is to wish you success and good luck!

Chapter four

The school as a business

Utilising school facilities

1. Summer schools

It is logical to make maximum use of the school's facilities and there is no reason why any school cannot seize the opportunity of earning extra revenue from them. Some schools have utilised outside organisations, such as tennis schools, cricket schools and football schools, leaving the entire organisation and administration to the business concerned. This is most definitely a possibility and the school need do little apart from open its gates and accept a cheque at the end of the exercise. A far more profitable way to proceed would be for the school to run its own summer schools. Many staff would relish the potential of being involved, but it is vital that there is no pressure to be involved. Consultation must occur at all times. Being of a purely educational nature, such activities are considered as primary purpose, and can be run as part of

the registered charity status of the school.
What options are available?
With a little thought, numerous possibilities come to mind: sports, drama, music, language laboratories, arts and crafts, ICT and graphic design. All are very adaptable to a summer school format. Exactly the same arguments apply to revision courses during the Easter break or on evenings during the summer term. It is very important that the school consults with maintenance staff, as it is often during the breaks from normal school activity that major maintenance work is conducted.

Administration
Experience has shown that it is advisable to have a common price structure and one booking form for all summer school classes. In order to prevent confusion, all administration should be carried out from one office and, if possible, by one individual. There will be numerous enquiries, especially during the first year that summer schools are pursued, so continuity of response is essential. Some schools have the advantage of boarding, and can market residential courses. No day school should be put off – local hotels are always interested in a deal, as they are when you are considering seminars and conferences for adults and corporate bodies. It is important to decide on dates relatively early, as many parents will want to start planning and booking holidays once Christmas is over.

There is little doubt that some may consider summer schools a glorified baby-sitting service. I can remember one eleven year-old child, the only offspring of two surgeons at the local hospital, actually attending eight successive weeks on courses. He progressed, over one weekend, from a week of ornamental Japanese pottery to Rugby on the Monday morning. As the individual running the Rugby course, I have to say that he was more suited to the pottery but, by the end of the week he acquitted himself well in the match played before the parents on the Friday afternoon. The courses must be marketed more as providing a constructive and creative input during the long summer breaks.

The public relations image of a caring school cannot be underestimated. Summer schools are popular with children immediately prior to starting senior school. It enables them to develop friendships and bond with future classmates before the more formal atmosphere of the school year gets underway.

Each course, mostly of one week duration, has a course director, whose responsibility is to determine staffing levels and run to budget. It is up to the director to recruit staff as appropriate and present a business plan to the management team. Fully qualified staff or helpers (sixth formers or undergraduates) can be recruited as numbers rise. It is important to note that the running of such courses should not be seen to impinge on normal teaching duties.

Following discussions with the heads of several schools, a teacher should do no more than one week during the Easter or summer break, or no more than one evening a week in the context of evening classes. All the staff involved are given a standard contract totally separate from their teaching contract. This should state the terms and conditions and a negotiated rate of pay, and it is made very clear to all that their responsibility covers looking after the children throughout the day, and all health and safety issues.

Catering for summer schools is another important consideration. The school can provide either a cooked meal or a sandwich but be aware that the majority of schools do not employ catering staff during the holidays. At one school, the course director calls at the local supermarket for a selection of pasties, pies and sandwiches to feed her charges during the day. Alternatively, the children can be asked to bring packed lunches. Be aware that children's packed lunches will vary considerably from the hamper to the plastic bag.

Budget
The budget is the responsibility of the course director. It must include any consumables (including lunch, if provided), marketing and publicity (usually common to all courses), nursing cover and ancillary staff requirements. There is obviously a threshold of course members that must be reached before the course can happen and various further thresholds before other staff can be recruited.

VAT is not applicable on course fees as long as they are aimed solely at children and are, in any way, considered to be of an educational nature. If adults are enrolled on courses, VAT becomes an issue. As an example of this, at Bolton we ran golf driving lessons across the school's pitches during July and August, with a professional, splitting the profits between the professional and the school. When we enrolled adults we had to charge VAT.

There are always going to be some difficulties when outsiders use school facilities, but profits realised from summer school activities can, potentially, lead to the acquisition of new equipment. A little tact and diplomacy with staff can lead to a minimising of any problems. There will be some staff who are not particularly interested. To the young teacher with a young family, there can be the added incentive of extra pay that could contribute much needed funds to the family annual holiday.

2. Commercial lettings
As with taking on summer schools, this subject must not be entered into lightly. It is vital to state that a school is primarily in existence to teach children in a normal working day and this function must have priority over any other. Many schools do use their facilities to let to outside organisations. To those schools who are registered charities, care must be exercised in that, as such, trading is not allowed

The School Fundraiser

Perhaps the best way to discuss lettings of facilities is to enumerate the experiences of one school as a case study. Bolton School is one of the largest independent day schools in the country, with 2,300 children between the age of two months and eighteen years. I mention two months as the latest venture is actually a crèche. This has been purpose built and will house eighty children when working to full capacity. It is calculated that after four years the setting up costs will be paid off and the nursery will be contributing £100,000 per annum back to the school.

The school is a beautiful architectural building set in thirty two acres and offers ideal surroundings and facilities to the local community. The indoor sports hall and swimming pool are let extensively along with the outdoor pitches. The school has recently set up an arrangement with Bolton Wanderers Academy of Youth Football for them to use the facilities, both for outdoor fixtures and indoor training. This is an excellent example of a business partnership that will be discussed later.

Several years ago the school recognised the potential of running the scout minibuses to certain areas around school that were somewhat difficult to reach by public transport. This was strongly influenced by the fact that children attending independent schools do not receive any subsidy on public transport. This initial exercise has now grown to a fleet of school coaches and over 1,100 children each day being transported to school at cheaper rates to the parents than utilising public transport or hiring other coach operators. It was quickly realised that these coaches should not be left idly sitting around when not in use by the school. They are now positively marketed to the surrounding area stressing experience in handling children. All running costs of the coaches are covered by the company while the school derives a good reliable service and an excellent marketing tool with which to attract potential parents. Obviously, very careful consideration should be given before embarking on such a scheme. Some schools have decreased any potential depreciation of coaches by adopting a similar approach using lease vehicles.

One of the first buildings on the present site of the school is a building designed and built as a swimming pool in 1905. Bolton was one of the very first schools to have its own pool. I have fond memories of this bath, of diving in at one end and banging your head on the other. By the mid eighties the pool had become redundant and had fallen into disuse. During the early nineties, the school recognised the potential and set up a successful appeal to convert it into a modern arts and conference centre.

While providing a superb venue for the children for the school play, dance and other activities, it is now rapidly becoming accepted as one of the premier venues for weddings, birthday parties, commercial exhibitions and concerts. A recent acquisition of a licence enables the wedding ceremony itself to be conducted at school as well. On a slightly sombre but bizarre note, there is a large crematorium just up the road and, though it is somewhat difficult to plan ahead, receptions after funerals are also being catered for at school.

Most schools have high levels of technology both regarding hardware and expertise. It is surprising how many people are keen to learn the latest about software. Courses on *Windows* and other software packages have proved most popular and everyone wants to learn more about the Internet. The language teaching facilities are also well used by the community with thirteen languages on offer mostly by self learning techniques. To schools recognised as centres of academic excellence, the opportunity of cramming courses also present themselves. An extremely well known independent school in Manchester recently offered its expertise in Oxford and Cambridge entry to the local state schools.

3. Outdoor education

Many schools now recognise the importance of outdoor pursuits, regarding both curricular and extra-curricular activities. There are many and varied centres where children and staff can utilise excellent facilities for these activities. At Bolton School the headteacher had the foresight to recognise the potential of this aspect and, with the backing of his governors, took out a lease on Patterdale Hall in the Lake District. The idea was not only to benefit his own children, but to open up the centre as a commercial operation when not being used by children from Bolton School.

Four years on into the development programme, the commercial programmes both for other schools and any other group of people cover the costs of running the whole operation. Many schools have such facilities all over the country, but not many have investigated the commercial opportunities. From a financial perspective, all these activities are operated by Bolton School Services Ltd, the commercial arm of the school. This is a trading company that Gift Aids its profits to the school at the end of each financial year. All full time and contracted staff at Patterdale Hall are employed by the company.

Patterdale Hall provides spacious facilities for groups while retaining many of the building's Victorian features. A certain amount of money has been invested in modernising and upgrading these facilities to meet current demands and regulations. The Hall specialises in providing reasonably priced, fully catered accommodation for up to sixty six people and can arrange transport using the fleet of modern coaches referred to above.

The programmes are aimed at those wishing to experience as many different activities as possible. They are also ideal for those experiencing the outdoors for the first time. All the activities used in the multi-activity programme take place in close proximity to the Hall and no travel is normally required. Some specialist programmes are designed to provide a greater experience of adventure and higher level of technical skill. They are ideal as a progression from a multi-activity programme, or for individuals who require coaching to an advanced level in a particular sport.

The centre can be marketed to other schools as the Hall is set in the ideal location for any residential course that includes direct links with everyday school work. A flexible approach enables the centre to be set up for very many different course needs. Options could include geography and biology field studies, GCSE sports modules, Duke of Edinburgh Award, Key Stages, understanding industry. The courses are designed to give individuals a head start in understanding the practical application of teamwork and leadership skills, providing them with a greater awareness as they progress to further education.

These courses can prove valuable for records of achievement and UCAS applications. Outdoor activities include sailing, kayaking, canoeing, fell walking and mountaineering, rock climbing, abseiling, caving, orienteering, gorge exploring, archery, ropes courses, initiative games, teamwork and leadership courses. All technical equipment and clothing appropriate for the activity is provided.

Today's business world requires an important contribution from management and staff training. Patterdale Hall provides a flexible approach to such needs and is marketed to the business sector in this way, always being aware that the requirements of the parent school have priority. Feedback has indicated a positive response from company members receiving these experiences. A selection of activities can provide a stimulating and relaxing break from the boardroom. Modern, newly developed conference facilities at the adjacent

Glenridding Hotel, combined with fresh air and outdoor activity, blend to provide a very successful venue. The ethos is to develop and deliver courses that are relevant to needs – moving away from buzz words and flip charts.

The practical issues of leadership and effective teamwork are addressed through the participation in relevant outdoor sports. In practical terms, the group embarks on an adventurous expedition where the team will be faced with real management and decision-making situations – but in an area that is different to their work environment. Time and again this approach has been shown to be tremendously successful in helping individuals and teams realise their full potential.

Activities now reach further afield using the mobile facilities. Expeditions can include an open canoe expedition crossing Scotland from Fort William to Inverness, a week of white water adventure canoeing or a week telemark/ski mountaineering in the Cairngorm mountains. A 45ft sail training vessel will be running a complete programme of sailing expeditions.

As can be seen, a relatively small operation has grown rapidly. The greatest care is taken over all aspects of safety. The outdoor instructors are experts in their field and provide the right balance of excitement, adventure and fun, as well as developing awareness and skill level in a large number of activities. Finally the commercial aspects of the centre provide income to support the running of a facility, which is a tremendous marketing tool for the school and offers all that the children need.

4. Business partnerships

Educational institutions are constantly seeking originality in that they source new areas of funding. Previous sections have demonstrated how schools can utilise their facilities for commercial gain. Provided the education of the students is given the highest priority, many varied facilities can be opened up. This can be only the very first step in creating symbiotic partnerships with local business, with both partners benefiting from such an arrangement.

All additional support generated should be used to extend the teaching and learning opportunities available. New technologies, particularly in the field of IT and communications have created a wide range of learning experiences. These technologies are expensive and require considerable investment, and while additional funding is now available from the government, schools need to be able to supplement this themselves. Improvements made possible by philanthropic and commercial support will not only stimulate the students to greater achievements but, also, will encourage parents to send their children to those schools.

It is wonderful to hear of gifts to schools and, in particular, those schools that have recently benefited form charitable bequests. Though there will always be true philanthropists, those who give large amounts for the betterment of others, we appear to be a nation that increasingly wants something back. Even philanthropy has been recently defined as self endeemed interest. This is particularly apparent from a study of charitable high street collections and the tried and tested house-to-house operations. There is now a quid pro quo element in giving, exemplified by the flowers or flags given away or the sale of the *Big Issue* magazines. Alternatively, we are constantly tempted to enter competitions or partake in lotteries in the hope, or even promise, of a financial return for our donation. One has to admire charities for constantly adapting and introducing innovative and original ideas in their attempts to persuade us to put our hands in our pockets.

Along similar lines, many schools are now thinking long and hard at what sort of benefits they can offer in return for promises of support. The answer is that schools are in a wonderful position to be able to do just that. Unlike many charitable organisations, schools, by their very nature, have the very best in sports and facilities. Schools can enter into valuable alliances with key contractors or suppliers, thereby strengthening business partnerships that clearly benefit both partners. Most schools are in close proximity to local restaurants who would be eager to have access to the school family as potential clients. Some schools have entered into a partnership involving a promotion where the restaurant donates money to the school for every meal booked under the promotion. At an Indian restaurant close to one school, the proprietor gave 25% of his takings over specific times to any individuals booking a table who specified that it was on behalf of the school promotion. The school actually benefited by over £2,000.00 The restaurant proprietor gains the benefit of a mailing with the school newsletter and an increased list of clientele. Both parties are very happy.

A wonderful example of such a partnership comes from a state school in south Manchester, Parrs Wood High School. A leaking building constructed in the sixties is situated on a prime development site on one of the major routes into the city. Following lengthy negotiations, a developer has agreed to build a new school in return for being allowed to create hotel, restaurant and leisure facilities on the old school site. The school will utilise its new facilities to create further partnerships with the local community. Arrangements with a group of solicitors see the school benefiting from any business from the school family. A local film producer will offer opportunities in media training in response to being allowed access to space in which to develop a studio. A long standing arrangement with ICL will see a major contribution of computer technology to the school over ten years, with useful research data being compiled for the company.

Thanks to the business partnership with Bolton Wanderers, Bolton School has benefited from a new irrigation system. A well known photographer, Paul Yaffe, has been allowed to approach the school family to encourage studio sittings. For every booking made, the school benefits financially. A group of local solicitors is regularly using the seminar facilities for their meetings. A long standing partnership with an international company enables the company to use the school's self-training facilities in order to train corporate staff in languages spoken where the company has foreign offices, as well as training visiting personnel in English.

For a successful partnership, any mutual arrangement must benefit both parties, and certainly schools can be in a strong bargaining position due to their physical assets, history and position within a community. In finalising such partnerships, much depends on the skill of the negotiator in these circumstances. Time and energy must be inputted to create lasting long term relationships with potential partners. These do not suddenly happen overnight and schools must be prepared to work hard to establish the trust necessary to initiate long and lasting business partnerships.

In all cases where there is the potential of a business benefiting from its relationship with a school or a charity, the law requires a written agreement called a Commercial Participators Agreement. This all originated when the charity – The World Wildlife Fund (WWF) entered into an agreement with Swan Vesta matches. As a result, for every box of matches that was sold, the company gave 1p to the charity. The charity and others looked at this and thought, how do we know that a business is not benefiting from a supposed association with a good cause? As a result the Charities Act 1992 incorporated a provision for the Commercial Participator's Agreement. An example of the outlines of such an agreement is set out below.

It is suggested that such an agreement is set up with any potential business that can be seen to be benefiting in any way from its association with the school. This can even

A commercial participator's agreement

This agreement made on the .... 20 ....

between

(1) .... School ....
Registered Charity No. .... (the School)

and

(2) .... (The Business)
 (the Commercial Participator)

Witnesses as follows:

1. Introduction
1.1 .... School is an institution existing for the education of children.

1.2 .... is a well established and well known business and is accepted by the School as being a suitable business with which to associate.

1.3 .... has an interest in the future development of the College and has a very high opinion of the School as an academic institution and a focal point within the community.

1.4 Preliminary discussions have taken place between .... on behalf of the School and .... following an initial approach by ...., leading to finalisation of the specific details below.

1.5 By an Agreement of even date herewith and made between the School and .... the latter will donate a percentage of profit resulting from business accrued from the School referrals, over a fixed period, to the School.

2. Operation
2.1 The School will promote the offer of support and the nature of the business of the Commercial Participator to the school "family".

2.2 Provided business accrued states, in advance, that it is referred from the School, the business will donate a percentage of their profits to the School.

2.3 Details of the offer will be circulated to:
a) all teaching staff
b) all past-pupils on the database
c) all parents of current children
d) general public in surrounding area
e) all local media representatives including newspapers and local radio.

3. Period of Agreement

3.1 This Agreement will expire on the completion of the allotted time period, accrual of all related income and all expenditure to the satisfaction of both parties.

4. Termination

4.1 The Agreement may be varied by mutual agreement.

4.2 Either party may have the option to terminating this Agreement without notice in the event of either party being in breach of any of the terms hereof.

5. Detailed Provisions

5.1 The business will donate between 1% and 20% dependant on the nature of the particular business accrued.

5.2 The offer will apply initially for a period of twelve months.

5.3 Proceeds will be donated provided business is accrued specifying that it is in aid of the School.

5.4 All bills issued to clients relating to the Agreement will be available for perusal by a representative of the School if so requested.

6. General

6.1 Neither party shall without the written consent of the other during or after the currency of the Agreement disclose any confidential information relating to the other which is acquired as a result of the Commercial Participator's involvement with the College PROVIDED ALWAYS that the Commercial Participator shall be at liberty to use as it thinks fit any general marketing intelligence in pursuance of the Agreement.

6.2 Whether or not this Agreement has been terminated, neither party will take legal proceedings for the enforcement of the terms of the Agreement or of any rights arising under it, without first having taken positive steps to resolve the matter by negotiation, mediation or other informal method of dispute resolution not involving publicity.

6.3 It is intended that this Agreement will be executed on the School's behalf by two properly authorised officers of the School.

6.4 Any notice to be served pursuant to this Agreement shall be served by recorded delivery in an envelope addressed to the other party at its last known address and such notice shall be deemed to have been received within four days of posting.

6.5 This agreement may not be amended by either party without the written consent of the other party.

6.6 This Agreement shall be governed by and construed in accordance with the laws of England.

Signed .... on behalf of .... (the School)

Date ....

Name ....

Signed .... on behalf of .... (the School)

Date ....

Name ....

Signed .... on behalf of .... (the Business)

Date ....

Name ....

be extended to benefits of a PR nature.

5. Sponsorship

Schools are very fortunate in having groups of people such as parents' or friends' associations who, as volunteers, are prepared to put a great deal of effort into organising fundraising events. The potential of sponsorship can add to the much needed funds in support of the school, no matter how big or how experienced in raising money they may be. As a biologist and member of the Institute of Biology, I turn to the natural world for a definition of sponsorship. Sponsorship has to be seen as a symbiotic relationship in existence for the mutual benefit of both parties. When considering sponsorship partners, it is essential to give much thought to what you can give back and, if such an offer from the school places the school in a unique bargaining position. To a business considering a sponsorship deal, there are multiple opportunities. In many cases the major factor is one of marketing. In other words, how many people will be aware of the business and what they do?

A very useful publication is the Hollis *Sponsorship & Donations Yearbook*, which is a guide to the UK's sponsorship and donating companies, plus sponsorship opportunities, specialist consultants and services. This contains a complete section on education. Further details are available from Harlequin House, 7 High Street, Teddington, Middlesex.

Probably the most important aspect of sponsorship is an awareness of what is ethically correct and what are the moral and legal standards that need to be applied. In the constant search for financial help, schools should be aware of the cute businessman seeking an opportunity to reach a new audience. With due respect to the many reputable companies and individuals involved in the industry, there are some people who would love to be able to approach your parents with offers of double glazing deals, time share or financial services. Be aware of the Data Protection Act, which prohibits your giving away lists of parents or old boys. The Advertising Standards Board and the National Consumer Council both have codes of practice that are worth investigating before proceeding with sponsorship deals.

Here are several examples of sponsorship deals, without referring to the particular school involved. These examples are taken from a number of my clients within both the state and independent sectors.

Case 1. A school well known as having an excellent football team receives sponsorship as a complete set of kit with sponsor's name on shirts. Just like premier league teams, the same principles apply. If the team does well, the company receives high profile. This particular school team reached the final of the Independent Schools Cup, so guaranteeing good exposure to a retail sports outfitter as sponsor.

Case 2. Along similar lines a state school reached a sponsorship deal with a well known local photographer who not only received exposure on the shirts, but was able to exhibit his contribution to the community with a framed photograph of the team in his studio.

Case 3. A school was able to negotiate a package with a large computer hardware supplier in exchange for a large number of PCs. The company was given the opportunity of researching teaching methods in the school over a period of time and, hence, enhancing its own marketing and sales techniques to the education sector.

Case 4. A company keen to produce good marketing literature in supplying science laboratory equipment provided some specialised equipment in exchange for the opportunity of photographing their product in a school environment. Similar examples to this are known with outdoor pursuits equipment companies, musical instrument manufacturers, ski equipment suppliers, self learning language equipment, overhead projection, and a variety of other teaching aids.

A little imagination and business acumen will open a number of doors.

Sponsorship need not necessarily be of a tangible nature. The feel good factor can often be exploited by schools to obtain financial benefit.

Case 5. An independent school keen to replace the Assisted Places scheme in an attempt to create bursaries, created a plan, as have many hospital and charitable appeals with Buy a Brick, or named chairs. Brass plaques were placed on chairs in the school hall with an ex-pupil's name and years at school. This created a form of immortality to past pupils, plus a chance of leaving something behind. In some cases grateful parents bought these as a way of saying thank you. A tremendous number of possibilities arise, such as wall plaques, commemorative books, tiles on the wall or floor, or even specific library books.

Case 6. A local manufacturing company helped a school to gain positive PR in their employer/employee relationships again, as above, demonstrating their contribution to the community from where their workforce was drawn, publishing the facts in their in-house magazine and overall giving a warm feel good factor to all their employees.

I could give many more examples of schools that have benefited considerably from sponsorship deals. If parent or ex-pupil groups become disenchanted by companies trying to elicit financial gain at all costs from sponsors, this can only damage relationships. Be aware that schools registered as charities cannot seek tax advantages from sponsorship deals as the sponsor is seen to be gaining a benefit from the agreement, thus making it unacceptable as a charitable donation.

Every school should seek full details of parental and ex-pupils' employment, enter them on the relationship database, and organise presentations to selected groups describing the wonderful advantages sponsorship can give to a company entering into a deal with the school.

6. School uniforms and shops

Many schools have considered the possibility of running a profitable business for their uniform sales with varying degrees of success. In some schools, PAs have taken responsibility and in others two or three individuals have decided to deal directly with the supplier. However, those who have tried this route will be aware of the problems that can be encountered. Perhaps the biggest problem is one of stock control. To the stock controller, the biggest nightmare presents itself with all sizes having to be readily available.

An alternative option is to set up a partnership with a business specialising in this aspect. F R Monkhouse Limited of Cheadle Hulme in Cheshire are one such business. There are others who offer a similar service but I shall concentrate on this company as I have worked closely with them for a number of years. They supply some four hundred schools in various ways. Sadly, many outfitters have closed in recent years due to the seasonal nature of the schoolwear trade, together with the problem of financing the year-round stocktaking. F R Monkhouse Ltd operate Intersport sports shops in addition to school wear, giving the company a much broader base. Sport provides an ideal running-mate with school wear, and also helps to maximise potential sales in school shop operations. Alongside these operations the business operates computer controlled embroidery equipment giving flexibility to badged garments. They also specialise in trophy supply and engraving, racket stringing, graphic design and printing, thus being in a position to offer a complete package.

School shops on-campus
F R Monkhouse Ltd operates an on-campus shop and covers all operating costs, stock, buying, staffing and management. The school provides the secure accommodation. Some of the shops provide sports equipment, tuck and stationery too. In many schools they are the supplier or have specific selling days at the school. The school shop option suits larger schools, those with a very distinctive uniform or boarding schools drawing from a wide geographic area.

These shops are run on a partnership basis with the schools concerned, the school supplying the secure accommodation package and the company taking responsibility for staffing, stocking and everything else at their expense. The school shop is often seen as the focus for all the school's retail activities and so bringing to an end various small departmental retailing activities that often take place.

While these may be well intentioned, they are often difficult to control. Those schools considering an on-campus retail outlet may well do so as much for an enhanced service to parents as for the income it provides. Schools already operating school shops themselves often find that the financial and management burdens are disproportionate to the financial returns. It is always worth talking to people already involved in the field. After all, it costs nothing to talk.

Responsibility of the company
- Shop planning. Where it should, and most importantly, where it should not be sited; siting of the school shop is most important as it requires easy access during the busiest period when the school itself may be closed. The company should produce drawings showing any

proposed lay-out of the shop interior.
- Shop fitting. The company undertakes all the shop fitting works, storage and display fixtures and counters. A company experienced in this field usually employs a system of shop fitting that is attractive yet functional, for school shops.

- Staff selection. Again, company experience has most likely included the ideal staff profile, contracts and job descriptions. It is important to have the involvement of the school during interviewing. The school should always retain the power of veto as there is no doubt that the conduct of the staff in the shop most often reflects upon the school itself.

- Product range. The shop will stock the complete range of uniform items required by pupils and, in addition, a range of ancillary sports items. In some cases there can also be stationery, tuck and school memorabilia. In the case of tuck, however, the greatly extended opening hours and the cost of this negates the profit element and more often than not, commission will not be paid on these sales.

- Quality and price. It is always wise to set certain standards on this aspect. I was amazed recently to be involved with a school that had three different suppliers of uniform all of different quality and price. The "better off" children were to be seen wearing the more quality garment, thus completely negating the whole point of having a levelling uniform for all children.

- Opening hours and staffing costs. Opening hours will be governed by demand and whether or not tuck is sold, but play a vital part in profitability. Staffing costs should conform to established levels as a percentage of turnover. An optimum balance between staff costs and customer service must be found in each instance.

- Stock levels. These require constant monitoring to achieve an acceptable stock turn ratio.

- Retail systems. All the forms and systems needed to run smoothly are supplied by the company.

- Credit cards. The company will install and pay the ongoing rental and commission charges associated with the electronic terminals.

Responsibility of the school
The school provides the secure accommodation package. This should be a suitably situated room of the appropriate size, carpeted and decorated. There should be physical and electronic security and a direct clean telephone line for data transmission.

- Carpeting, decorating and lighting. Carpeting in a school shop needs to be of durable nature and colour –carpet tiles give low cost, long life and interchangability in the event of an accident or a wear path developing. Decorating need be no more than emulsion paint to walls and gloss to woodwork. Lighting needs to be to a rather higher level than normal, as school wear tends to absorb light.

- Security. It is absolutely essential that the shop has both physical protection and electronic security. The physical protection should provide a deterrent to the would-be thief and slow the entry down sufficiently to allow time for the alarm to be effective. Bars or grills are almost certainly going to be an insurance stipulation. A modern break-glass detector will give electronic protection to all the glass within its listening range and PIRs (passive infra-red detectors) will give excellent space protection at modest cost. Insurers now insist upon NACOSS approved installers, Red Care telephone line monitoring and a central station alarm

monitoring service.
- Commission. F R Monkhouse Ltd states that the school receives a commission of 10% on all the school wear and sports sales from the school shop paid quarterly. It is anticipated that the company will achieve a similar or slightly greater net profit from the operation in line with the level of work involved. As a partnership operation, it is only correct that the financial side of the operation is transparent and the school may have sight of the profit and loss account.

In-school sales operations
This is an excellent way in which to derive commission on the pre-September term sales, which will be approximately 60% of the annual total. The company conduct a new-intake sales operation, or sell within the school and pay a commission on these sales. This would usually take place in June or July. The company undertakes the printing of price lists, order forms and provides staff on the selling day(s). A little assistance from school staff or parents' association may be useful. A year-round replacement garment service is available from a nearby retail branch, but without commission on those later sales. Replacement items can also be supplied on a mail-order basis. This option is particularly suited to high schools without a particularly distinctive uniform and to those schools some distance from the nearest school wear branch. The school is not involved in any stockholding or cash handling and has no financial risk whatsoever.

PTA partnerships
This is a variation of the above in school sell suited to schools distant from a school wear branch – distance is irrelevant. The company produces price lists and order forms which the parents association would, as an association project, distribute and subsequently collect from new-intake and existing parents. The PTA would send these along with the customers' cheques or credit card details to the company. The orders would be made

up in manpacks and returned to the school. The PTA would then be responsible for the distribution of these (paid) orders. Any exchanges of size that may be required would be dealt with later by means of a simple schedule of items returned and a schedule of items required. In the case of F R Monkhouse Ltd, the company would then send the PTA a cheque to the value of 10% of the gross value of the operation. The value could be in the region of £1,000 to £1,500 for an average high school.

Memorabilia
Some companies can supply a wide range of products that carry the school's crest. These are suitable for parents, grandparents and old boys or girls of the school. Items such as engraved glassware, wallets, pen and pencil sets, key rings and embroidered clothing are extremely popular with some people.

Wholesale – a one-stop solution
Schools that already have their own sales operation often find that the cost of maintaining buying and product sourcing skills within the school is simply not cost effective, bearing in mind the small scale of the operation. A characteristic would be out of balance stocks, uncompetitive prices being paid and potential quality problems. In short, an increasing problem for the bursar. Some companies act as consultants and can offer a simple one-stop solution to all school wear and sports purchasing. The prices paid may, in some cases, be a little higher than purchasing directly from the manufacturer but it is much easier and safer to use the experience and expertise of professionals in this very specialist area.

Appendix 1
Some useful addresses

Institute of Development Professionals in Education (IDPE)
PO Box 102, Manchester M14 6XE
Tel/Fax: 0161 434 1847
email: info@idpe.org.uk www.idpe.org.uk

Institute of Charity Fundraising Managers (ICFM)
Market Towers, 1 Nine Elms Lane, London SW8 5NQ
Tel: 0207 627 3436 Fax: 0207 627 3508

Association of Development Directors in Independent Schools (ADDIS)
ADDIS Secretariat, Sondes Barn, Patrixbourne, Canterbury, KENT CT4 5DD
Tel: 07000 623347 Fax: 01227 832265
email: 106210.16@compuserve.com

Council for Advancement and Support of Education (Case Europe)
Suite 21a, Tavistock House North, Tavistock Square, London WC1H 9HX
Tel: 0207 387 4404
email: schools2000@eurocase.org.uk

British Schools and Universities Foundation (BSUF)
Mrs S Wiltshire, Hon UK Representative, 6 Windmill Hill, Hampstead, London NW3 6RU.

Licensing Theatres & Concerts Performing Rights Society
29–35 Berners Street, London W1P 4AA

British Parachuting Association
Kimberley House, 47 Vaughan Way, Leicester LE1 4SG

British Mountaineering Council
Crawford House, Precinct Centre, Booth Street East, Manchester M13 0RL

Charity Commission
London Office: Harmsworth House, 13 – 15 Bouverie Street, London EC4Y 8DP
Tel: 0870 333 0124
Liverpool Office: 2nd Floor, 20 Kings Parade, Queens Dock, Liverpool L3 4DQ
Tel: 0151 703 1500

Scottish Charities Office
Crown Office, 25 Chambers Street, Edinburgh, EH1 1LA
Tel: 0131 226 2626

Northern Ireland Charities Branch
Department of Health and Social Services, Room C4, 22 Castle Buildings, Stormont, Belfast BT4 3PP
Tel: 01232 522780

HM Customs and Excise
New King's Beam House, 22 Upper Ground, London SE1 9PJ
Tel: 0207 620 1313

Inland Revenue Charity Division
St John's House, Merton Road, Bootle, Merseyside L69 9BB
Tel: 0151 472 6000

Charity Division for Scotland
FICO Scotland, Trinity Park House, South Trinity Road, Edinburgh EH5 3SD
Tel: 0131 551 8127

British Council
10 Spring Gardens, London SW1A 2BN
Tel: 0207 930 8466

Charities Aid Foundation
Kings Hill, West Malling, Kent ME19 4TA
Tel: 01732 520000
email: cafoubs@caf.charitynet.org www.charitynet.org

Data Protection Commissioner
Wycliffe House, Water Lane, Wilmslow, Cheshire SK9 5AF
Tel: 01625 545745

Directory of Social Change
24 Stephenson Way, London NW1 2DP
Tel: 0207 209 4949

Education Services
Rosegarth Associates, 101a Wellington Road, Withington,
Manchester M14 6AY
Tel: 0161 434 4808 Fax: 0161 434 1847
email: DPoppitt@aol.com

Law Society
113 Chancery Lane, London WC2A 1PL
Tel: 0207 242 1222

National Lottery Department
14 Great Peter Street, London SW1P 3NG
Tel: 0207 312 0123

National Council for Voluntary Organisations
Regent's Wharf, 8 All Saints Street, London N1 9RL
Tel: 0207 713 6161

Sports Council
16 Upper Woburn Place, London WC1H 0QP
Tel: 0207 273 1500

F R Monkhouse Limited
The Precinct, Cheadle Hulme, Cheshire SK8 5BE
Tel: 0161 486 1309 Fax: 0161 488 4432

Gaming Board for Great Britain
Berkshire House, 168 – 173 High Holborn, London WC1V 7AA
Tel: 0207 306 6200

Appendix 2
Useful reading

Poppitt, David G (1998) *Building Relations between Educational Establishments and Local Business* Journal of Nonprofit and Voluntary Sector Marketing Vol 3 No 2 pp 173 – 178

Smyth, Julian (1977) *Back to School? What the voluntary sector can learn from the education sector* Journal of Nonprofit and Voluntary Sector Marketing Vol 2 No 4 pp 365 – 372

Burnett, Ken (1992) *Relationship Fundraising* White Lion Press, London

Charitable Trends (1995) Charities Aid Foundation.

Needle, Paul and Stone, Merlin (1977) *Marketing for Schools* Croner Publications, London

Forrester, Susan, Mountfield, Anne and Patel, Alka (eds) (1995) *The Education Funding Guide* Directory of Social Change

The Directory of Grant Making Trusts – Focus Series Schools Colleges and Educational Establishments 1st Edition, Charities Aid Foundation

Fundraising for Education How To series, Charities Aids Foundation

Rosenberg, Harris *A Handbook of School Fundraising* (1998) Kogan Page Ltd, London

The Hollis Sponsorship & Donations Yearbook (published annually) Hollis Directories Ltd, Teddington, Middlesex

The Hollis UK Press Publications Annual (published annually) Hollis Directories Ltd., Teddington, Middlesex

Corporate Fundraising Ed Valerie Morton (1999) Charities Aids Foundation/ICFM Fundraising Series

Middleton, Fiona and Lloyd, Stephen (1993) *Charities – The New Law* Jordons & Sons Ltd., Bristol

Roberts, Tom (1999) *The Funding Revolution – New routes to Project Fundraising* Falmer Press, London

Blume, Hilary (1984) *Charity Christmas Cards* Charities Advisory Trust, London

Value Added Tax for Charities (1995) HM Customs and Excise VAT Leaflet 701/1

Charities and Fundraising CC20 & CC20(a), Charity Commissioners

Trading by Charities C52, Inland Revenue Charities Series

Eastwood, Nicola, Mountfield, Anne and Walker, Louise *The Schools Funding Guide* Directory of Social Change

Essential reading
for all school fundraisers...

Managing
Schools Today

As the UK's leading magazine for all those involved in primary and secondary school management, *Managing Schools Today* will offer you regular features on school fundraising. The magazine also provides you with comprehensive news and in-depth analysis, an essential teaching resource supplement, a guide to successful performance management and a school improvement 'soap opera'.

As well as providing you with the latest information and management practices to support you in your role, *Managing Schools Today* will also feature regular articles on good practice, lifestyle, personal development and a whole host more. This plus a selection of more light hearted reading will ensure that even when you just want to settle down to a relaxing read *Managing Schools Today* will be there to help you wind down, and to keep you in touch with the school management community.

Subscription Price: £48.00 per annum
Frequency: six issues a year
ISSN: 0968 1558

Credit Card Hotline: 0121 666 7878
Fax: 0121 666 7879

QUESTIONS
PUBLISHING

The Questions Publishing Company
321 Bradford Street
Birmingham
B5 6ET
www.education.quest.com

Further reading
for <u>all</u> school managers...

Professional Development *Today*

Professional Development Today is the indispensable journal covering all aspects of teacher training and professional development.

A sister publication to *Managing Schools Today*, *Professional Development Today* is designed to support all those involved in the personal and professional development of teachers. It explores such key topics as recruitment techniques, assessing teachers' skills, mentoring and enhancing teaching performance.

"The Government will support teachers, schools and the whole profession in a partnership of inclusive, high quality professional development. Such partnership is essential in developing the careers of teachers and improving standards in the classroom"

Estelle Morris MP

Special Offer –

A subscription to Professional Development Today is just £15.00 when you subscribe to Managing Schools Today – saving £10.00.

Each issue gives readers access to:

- Information on the latest initiative in professional development
- Detailed guidance on emerging practice and new approaches
- In depth interviews with leading practitioners and policy makers
- Concise reviews of the latest research

Credit Card Hotline: 0121 666 7878
Fax: 0121 666 7879

The Questions Publishing Company
321 Bradford Street
Birmingham
B5 6ET
www.education.quest.com

Subscription Price: £25.00
Frequency: three issues a year
ISSN: 1460-8340

www.ingramcontent.com/pod-product-compliance
Lightning Source LLC
Chambersburg PA
CBHW070628300426
44113CB00010B/1699